DEVON'S HERITAGE

Along the Shore

All photographs by Sandra Yeo except where stated

First published in 1984 by Badger Books, Bideford, North Devon
Typeset by Lens Typesetting, Bideford, North Devon.
Printed by Devon Print Group of Exeter.

ACKNOWLEDGEMENTS

I would like to express my grateful thanks to my wife, Elaine, who patiently read, edited and typed my manuscript. I am also grateful to Mervyn Baker, Mike Glover, Dennis Heard, John Jeffery, Sandra Yeo, Elaine Towns and the Nature Conservancy Council for kindly loaning the photographs for the book. Thanks too to all the people who over the years wittingly or unwittingly guided me to so many places of outstanding beauty and interest in North Devon.

MIKE TOWNS

Blackchurch Rock

From the broken, contorted rocks of Hartland to the vast sand-dunes of Braunton Burrows, and the towering cliffs of Exmoor, the North Devon coastline is breathtaking. Wild, windswept uplands and shattered cliffs pounded by Atlantic waves contrast with sweeping bays filled with golden sand and massive, plunging cliffs clothed in a green carpet of dense woodland. Here wildlife can be found in abundance, safe in the protection of inaccessible cliffs or marginal land unsuitable for agriculture.

North Devon's coastline is unknown Devon. Overshadowed by the magnificence of Dartmoor and of Exmoor, and by the much more widely known and acclaimed beauty of South Devon, it remains relatively unexplored. Yet this dramatic stretch of coast presents a spectacle unequalled anywhere in England.

This book is the result of many hours of happy exploration, and attempts to take the reader on a tour of discovery of the coastline and will, I hope, lead you to your own explorations along this truly splendid shore.

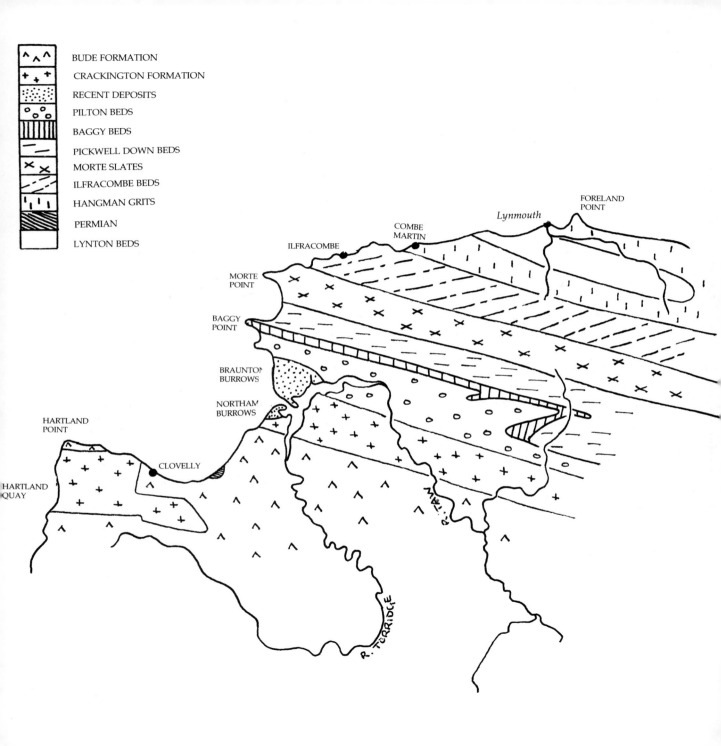

BUDE FORMATION

CRACKINGTON FORMATION

RECENT DEPOSITS

PILTON BEDS

BAGGY BEDS

PICKWELL DOWN BEDS

MORTE SLATES

ILFRACOMBE BEDS

HANGMAN GRITS

PERMIAN

LYNTON BEDS

FORELAND POINT

Lynmouth

COMBE MARTIN

ILFRACOMBE

MORTE POINT

BAGGY POINT

BRAUNTON BURROWS

NORTHAM BURROWS

HARTLAND POINT

HARTLAND QUAY

CLOVELLY

R. TORRIDGE

MIKE TOWNS is well fitted to write on the subject of North Devon's coast and shoreline, for he spends his working life caring for one section of it. Five years ago he was appointed Warden of the Northam Burrows Country Park. It is his job to care for this unique area of sand and marsh, protected only by the Pebble Ridge from the constant threat of reclamation by the sea, and to steer a smooth path between the needs of the various bodies who use the Burrows – the farmers, the naturalists, the riders, the golfers, and the holidaymakers. No easy task.

Before moving to North Devon, Mike Towns had an even harder task for he was the Conservation Warden for Milton Keynes Development Corporation – the huge new town in Buckinghamshire.

In his mid 30's, Mike is one of the few people who can claim to have been born within the sound of Bow Bells. Although his early life was spent in London, he was always interested in the countryside and wildlife, and remembers the turning point in his life. This occurred on a working holiday at Tunbridge Wells, his first real experience of large areas of natural country which he found irresistible. But it was a bee fly landing on his arm that really roused his curiosity and sent him off to the the local library to find out all about the insect. From then on he was hooked and today Mike confesses that although keenly interested in all wildlife, it is the spiders and all "creepy crawlies" that are his especial interest.

Cover photograph by Dennis Heard

Back Cover, Herring Gull   *John Jeffery*

5

Hartland to Westward Ho!

Rock formation at Hartland Quay

Struggling to remain on your feet in the teeth of a gale at Hartland Point brings home just why the Romans called this wind-blasted spot the 'Promontory of Hercules': at the same time, maybe only a dozen yards away, a kestrel hanging effortlessly motionless over the cliffs causes you to marvel at the ability of nature to fashion its creatures so skilfully to meet the challenges of their environment.

Exposed to the full force of Atlantic wind and sea, the coastline south from Hartland Point is a stunningly beautiful tangle of twisted rocks, vertical cliffs and jutting reefs. Off Hartland Point the tide surges and races through submarine reefs always ready to claim another victim from among the many vessels that pass the headland daily. To the east, in the curve of Bideford Bay, Clovelly

nestles in the lee of the Point, sheltered from the more devastating winds. Here well-grown woodlands clothe the steep slopes of the cliffs, their trunks and branches festooned with mosses and lichens that flourish in the moisture-laden air. Beyond Clovelly the wind once again reasserts its dominance, stunting the cliffside woodlands and building the massive wind-blown sand dunes of Braunton Burrows.

Hartland Point itself is a cap of resistant, blocky Culm sandstone affording protection to the more easily eroded rock layers of the Crackington Formation behind it. Both types of rock were deposited as silt and mud more than 300 million years ago when Devon lay at the bottom of an offshore sea. This was the Carboniferous era, better known as the Coal Age, a time of swamps, giant amphibians and lush tropical forests whose decayed remains eventually formed the coal we mine today. At Hartland Quay, as proof of their watery origin, some of the rock layers exposed by erosion bear clear and unmistakable fossil ripples on their surface. During their long history these submarine rocks sank into the bowels of the earth to be baked and hardened by the great heat of the interior. Later they were thrust back into the air, and twisted and folded to form a great chain of mountains. Over aeons of time these mountains eroded away to form a low, flat plain. This is the Devon of today. A plateau deeply dissected by young, fast-flowing rivers with only the worn stump of Dartmoor to remind us of the volcanoes and the mountains. Further upheaval was required to complete the character of the present day coastline – the great Ice Ages.

As the vast ice sheets that covered most of the northern hemisphere came and went, so the sea level rose and fell and the land was 'bounced' up and down. It is curious to think of land 'bouncing' – called isostasy by geologists – but the fantastic weight of ice, in places up to a mile thick, simply pressed the land slowly down into the Earth's crust. When the ice melted and the weight was removed, the land rose up once again. To this day Scotland continues to rise after the passing of the last Ice Age. One result of all this activity was that at times the sea lapped a shore up to 25 feet higher than it is today, while at others it withdrew many miles from our present shoreline. After the last Ice Age most of the streams along the coast of north-west Devon were stranded high up on the cliffs, with too meagre a water supply for them to vigorously cut down their beds to sea level. Instead the rising sea has eroded away the coast faster than the streams can carve their valleys and they have been left stranded high up on the cliffs and now fall to the sea-shore in spectacular waterfalls.

The most famous and most beautiful waterfall on the North Devon coast is that at Speke's Mill Mouth. The stream drops over a sheer wall of rock almost 60 feet high. It then tumbles a further 100 feet down a series of four smaller falls before it finally reaches the sea. There is another splendid fall at Windbury Point near Mouth Mill, but it is very difficult to reach on foot. Most visitors must content themselves with watching the waterfall from Mouth Mill beach, especially after rain when the water plumes to the shore in a long silver arc.

The wildlife of this coast is certainly equal to its grandeur. Hartland is the North Devon stronghold of the peregrine falcon, the fastest and most graceful of all birds of prey. There can surely be few greater thrills than the sight of a peregrine dropping out of the sky at speeds of up to 180 miles per hour in pursuit of its prey. Yet during the early 1960s this magnificent bird had disappeared from Cornwall and was all but extinct in Devon due to pesticide poisoning. The seed-eating birds that form the bulk of the peregrines' prey were accumulating poisonous chemicals in their bodies from the chemical dressings on the seeds they ate. When these contaminated birds were caught and eaten by the peregrines, the poisons they contained had devastating effects. The pesticides caused the female peregrines to lay thin-shelled eggs that were easily broken in the nest. Breeding success plummeted and gradually their population declined. Just in time the use of these destructive chemicals was severely restricted and the peregrine, along with other birds of prey similarly affected, has begun to recover its former abundance.

In the south-west peregrine nest-sites are virtually confined to the sea-cliffs of the coast. Eggs are laid in early April on rock ledges covered with soft earth. Occasionally they will use old ravens' nests and there is sometimes competition between the two species for the available nest sites. Before nesting a pair will indulge in breathtaking courtship flights; soaring, diving, sweeping sometimes singly, sometimes in concert – a truly remarkable display. At times the birds may touch talons or grasp bills in flight. During courtship the male regularly brings food for his mate, often passing it to her while in flight.

The raven, with whom the peregrine has an uneasy relationship, is another fascinating bird. Once it was widespread and common, following the plough in the countryside and scavenging on refuse and carcasses in cities. Now it lives primarily on the coast and in wild highland areas with its greatest populations in Wales and the south-west. It nests all along the North Devon coast and the birds form sizable flocks in the winter which may move inland at dusk to roost. The large size of the raven – it is as big as a buzzard, its kite-shaped tail and its deep, croaking call make it unmistakable. The raven also has the strange habit of momentarily flipping upside down as it flies, something readily seen when it flies below you as you walk the clifftop paths.

Ravens feed mainly on carrion but will eat a wide variety of food and can catch and kill small mammals and birds. Their habit of feeding on the bodies of men slain in battle has earned them a sinister and mystical reputation. A croaking bird flying overhead is an omen of misfortune in many places.

Other cliff-nesting birds are scarce along this part of the coast but there are several small colonies of herring gull and fulmar. If, in the

Gallantry Bower

Nesting Seabirds

8

spring, you have the stamina to embark on the long haul to Gallantry Bower from Brownsham or Clovelly you may be rewarded by coming eyeball-to-eyeball with a sitting gull or fulmar. An overgrown cliff-top path will lead you to an archway flanked by the true, scented Devon violets, and moschatel, an odd little plant with its flower heads forming a square blossom like the faces of 'the Town Hall clock', its common name. Once through the archway you stand on a balcony carved into the sheer rock face, the cliff dropping away from you a dizzying 300 feet to the seashore below. To the left and right herring gulls and fulmars sit on the rock ledges incubating their eggs and if you are lucky you may catch a glimpse of a young bird peering out from beneath its parent's wing. The fulmars are relatively recent arrivals to the Devon coast. Only a hundred years ago they were confined to the Shetland Islands but now they are colonising every suitable nesting site on the British coast and their stiff-winged, gliding flight is a familiar sight.

Silent by day, when the Manx Shearwater returns to its burrow at night it utters strange unearthly calls

Some other new arrivals to this coast are the divers which congregate off Hartland Point from January to March. In recent years large, mixed flocks of great northern, black-throated and red-throated divers have gathered regularly in these turbulent waters. They are most easily observed in calm weather – unfortunately all too rare here – but a telescope is really essential for the best views. Occasionally they will come closer inshore and great northern divers have been seen for several winters off Mouth Mill and in the waters of the Taw/Torridge estuary.

Another notable feature is the mass movement of Manx shearwaters past the Point between April and September. They pass in their thousands, in the early morning heading for their open sea feeding grounds and returning during the late evening, reaching their nest burrows on uninhabited islands off the Welsh coast after dark. Because they are clumsy and vulnerable on land their nocturnal and burrowing habits spare them from the attentions of predators, particularly the larger gulls.

Great Northern Diver. Dives for fish, sometimes travelling long distances underwater and staying submerged for up to a minute

9

During spring and autumn there is also a steady movement of migrating song birds, though Hartland Point is not so good for passerine watching as are Morte Point or Baggy Point. However, siskin are often seen during October and November and pied flycatchers, ring ousel and yellow wagtail are regular visitors. One species particularly worth mentioning is the black redstart. This small, rusty-tailed, sooty-grey bird can be found in the area throughout most of the winter. Only a few tens of pairs breed in Britain, mostly in the east, and the majority of British birds move south to the Continent during winter but some remain in the south-west. The open, grassy cliffs and short, wind-stunted scrub of this coast seems to suit them admirably. One other place where they can be seen regularly during passage is the seaside resort of Westward Ho! Here they hop about, constantly flicking their orange tails, among the closed amusement arcades and on the deserted promenade.

The breezy cliff-top grasslands of the Hartland coast support a variety of interesting plant species, some of them scarce and local. From March to May the cliff paths are heady with the scent of gorse, the grass speckled with the white flowers of the early scurvy grass, the yellow primroses and the beautiful, clear, pale blue stars of the spring squill – a very local plant confined to the sea coasts of the west. Scurvy grass is not a grass at all but a small flowering plant with succulent leaves. Two kinds occur on these cliffs; the early scurvy grass which often appears as a minute dwarf form clinging to the crumbling edges of the cliffs, and the common scurvy grass which is a larger plant flowering later in the year. Early scurvy grass, while relatively common on the west coast, is rare in the rest of Britain. It is a speciality of the north-west Devon coast

and at times grows in astonishing profusion. The name scurvy grass derives from its ability to relieve or cure scurvy – the age-old pestilence of seafarers. The plant is rich in vitamin C and before citrus fruits were known and became widely available scurvy grass was carried on ships as dried bundles of leaves to be infused as tea, or as a tonic wine made from the juices of the fresh leaves. Tonic wine was by far the most popular form of administration because it masked the sometimes bitter taste of the plant. Although very much a coastal plant, in this corner of Devon common scurvy grass also occurs abundantly in hedgebanks on roadsides, presumably having escaped from cottage gardens where it was grown for its medicinal properties.

As spring passes into summer there is a fresh display of colour. Pink cushions of thrift perch on every available ledge and compete for attention with the yellow flowers of kidney vetch and the white flowers of sea campion and wild carrot. All these seaside plants are remarkable for their ability to resist the shrivelling power of salt. Over one hundredweight of salt per acre is deposited on the cliff tops each year, most of it as salt spray blown in from the sea by winter storms. Many species are succulent, holding extra water in their cells to buffer the effects of the salt. Remarkable too is the fact that many of our modern vegetables were bred from these succulent and salt-tolerant plants. Cabbage, kale and beetroot all have their origins in their maritime counterparts and the garden carrot with its fleshy taproot was bred from the stringy-rooted Mediterranean form of the sea carrot.

The actual cliff flora along the north-west coast is, however, relatively poor. The upright strata of the Bude Formation rocks are

Rock Strata, Blackchurch Rock, Mouthmill

The Gore, Bucks Mills,

liable to fall and sweep away any accumulated soil and the Crackington Formation, due to its shaly nature, is easily eroded, readily slipping and crumbling into the sea. All along the coast there are regular landslips and old and new scars can be seen everywhere. One most spectacular example of the amount of material that can fall from the cliffs in a single landslip is the Gore at Bucks Mills. This spit of Culm Measures sandstone roughly 500 ft wide and 1500 ft long, extends out to sea in a narrow triangle. The word 'gore' means both 'triangle-shaped' and 'rocks piercing a ship' and, given the notorious nature of this coast, both terms are very apt. The Gore is composed of large boulders, none of them less than two feet wide, and the belief is that this is all that remains of a massive landslip which occurred probably several hundred years ago – a chart dated 1795 has the Gore clearly marked. The smaller boulders would have

been washed out and transported along the shore by the sea. These crumbly cliffs also sit astride the geologically active Sticklepath Fault – there was an earthquake on this fault in the Okehampton area in 1858 – which makes for considerable instability.

These slippages are not all bad, however. The eroding cliffs and disturbed ground provide niches for the fringed or ciliated pearlwort and the sea storksbill. Both are scarce, the fringed pearlwort particularly so. Here, too, is the coltsfoot, now a common and pernicious garden and waste ground weed. Yet once, when Britain was largely covered in forest, it must have been rare. Perhaps it survived then on crumbling cliffs like these, waiting for any opportunity to spread. The Latin name for the coltsfoot, *Tussilago,* means 'cough plant' and it was indeed used for centuries as a cough cure. In fact, even today, if you buy some of the more famous patent cough medicines you will find that 'extract of Tussilago' is a vital ingredient. The common name coltsfoot refers to the shape of the leaves.

As the coast sweeps round from Hartland the clifftop grasslands give way more and more to windswept scrub. Dense mats of gorse, blackthorn, willow and privet clothe the cliffs, providing ideal nesting sites for stonechats, linnets and whitethroats. The whitethroat, despite its skulking habits, is generally well known and is unmistakable when it perches atop a bush to deliver its chattering song, its white throat shining in the sunlight.

The valleys that slice through the cliffs to the sea provide sufficient shelter for woodland to grow. The ribbons of woodland at Brownsham and Mouth Mill are the most extensive but they have been sadly depleted by felling and conversion to monocultures of exotic conifers – largely Sitka spruce and Douglas fir. Both these conifers have silver stripes beneath their needles but the Sitka spruce is sharp and spiny while the needles of the Douglas fir are soft and give off a striking

Coltsfoot

scent of oranges when crushed. Here and there a giant silver fir, spared from felling, towers over the plantations, usually with its top broken out due to its sudden and rude exposure to the elements.

At Brownsham some of the woodland and several marshy fields have been set aside as a nature reserve managed by the Devon Trust for Nature Conservation. The reserve is a marvellous mixture of young and old woods and rush-covered fields, but its most fascinating feature is a tree library. Local reserve volunteers have fenced off an otherwise uninteresting part of a field and planted a whole range of native tree and shrub species which can be found in the British Isles. The idea is to create a living library that schoolchildren and naturalists can visit to learn the recognition of our common and not so common trees and shrubs.

Sea Storksbill

Badgers abound in the valley woods where they search for snails and blackberries or dig for bluebell bulbs. From the fields they take mainly earthworms, surprisingly small prey for such large and powerful creatures. You'll be lucky to see one but you may come across their dung pits at the edges of woods and fields. These are shallow holes dug a few yards apart by badgers, into which they deposit their droppings. Dung pits are territory markers and may sometimes extend for a hundred yards or more. Unfortunately, Hartland is an area where bovine tuberculosis is rife and in consequence the local badgers have been savagely persecuted, despite the fact that the role of the badger in causing or maintaining the disease has yet to be proven conclusively. There is evidence that earthworms and other soil creatures are capable of transmitting the disease and many wild mammals other than badgers have been found infected. It could well be that the infected cattle pass on the disease to wildlife rather than the reverse. The badger's only crimes are that it is big, easily studied, readily infected and comparatively easy to kill.

Badger

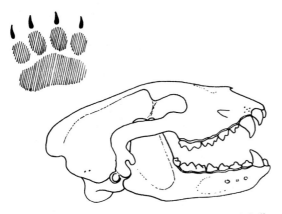
Badger's footprint and skull

On reaching Clovelly the coast finally becomes sheltered enough to grow woodlands of tall oaks and ash, most of it clinging to the perilously steep slopes of the Hobby Drive, so steep in places that the canopy is almost at eye level. The oaks are mainly the sessile or durmast oak, the oak of upland and western regions. It has long-stalked, leathery leaves and stalkless acorns. There are few undershrubs in these woods, just a tangled layer of bramble, fern and thick beds of the grass-like wood rush, *Luzula campestris*. This is ideal territory for the wood warbler which builds its domed nest of bracken, grass and dead leaves on the floor of the wood. The wood warbler is not a shy bird and is easily seen, its greenish back and yellow breast contrasting with its white underparts. They are very common at the Hobby Drive and every few hundred yards they can be seen and heard uttering their loud, distinctive, trilling song. A mixture of other trees such as beech and sweet chestnut have been planted on the more accessible slopes and rowan is a common pioneer and understorey tree. However, the interest of these woods lies not

Woodlands and Tree Lichens

only in the trees but also in the tremendous variety of lichens that clothe the trunks and festoon the branches. Because of the richness of the lichen flora the Hobby Drive has been designated a Site of Special Scientific Interest and as such receives special protection under the Wildlife and Countryside Act.

Lichens are beneficial associations between fungi and algae (microscopic green plants). Both partners in this association are extremely rare or unknown as separate, free-living plants but together they form the marvellous variety of lichens that grow on bare rock as well as soil or shrubs and trees. The algae, through their chlorophyll, provide the sugars needed to sustain the plant and the fungi provide the shell to house the algae and are responsible for the thousands of wonderful shapes of the lichens. Lichens also absorb some nutrients from the surface they grow on and from rainfall and for this reason they are highly sensitive to air pollutants, particularly sulphur dioxide vented from factory chimneys. Apart from the area around the CEGB power station at Fremington – which is due to close soon – North Devon is relatively free of heavy industry and the air, swept in across hundreds of miles of ocean, is clean and pure. In consequence the lichen flora is rich and varied and the ancient, largely unmanaged woodlands of the sea coast house rare species otherwise found only in the clean air regions of Scotland and west Wales. Among the more conspicuous and rarer lichens are the 'beard lichens' *(Usnea species)* that hang from trunks and branches in strings and bunches up to a yard long. *Usnea articulata* is the longest-growing species, often likened to a string of sausages, each 'sausage' up to a quarter of an inch wide. This is the *Usnea* species most sensitive to air pollution. Where it was once common – it even grew in London – it is now extinct and at present can be found only in south-west England. *Usnea ceratina* is another very long species, but without the 'sausages'; it is more pollution tolerant and widely distributed in the south. The most beautiful of the beard lichens is *Usnea florida*. It grows in short tufts capped with large, fringed discs (ascocarps), up to half an inch wide, that look uncannily like grey-green flowers, hence the Latin name 'florida'.

As well as hanging from branches, lichens also encrust the trunks of trees, at times so much so that it is impossible to find the bark beneath. The large, circular, grey-green, almost luminous patches of the *Parmelia* lichens always draw attention and around them, jostling for space, grow a wide variety of thin and papery, or thick and leafy lichens. On smooth-barked trees, such as young ash or rowan, are commonly found what I like to call the 'writing lichens'. These are white, paper-thin lichens that could easily be mistaken for the bark of the tree, but over their surface are numerous dark, elongated fruit bodies that can look very much like Oriental script. There are two main groups, *Opegrapha,* which has long, squiggly, close-packed fruit bodies and *Graphis* which has smaller, simpler fruit bodies.

In the past quite a few lichens had practical uses. A number of species yield very good dyes; *Usnea florida* was a source of glucose for conversion to alcohol and in Scandinavia a number of *Usnea* species are the source of a powerful antibiotic. Probably the best known medicinal lichen, which was once common over much of Britain, is the tree lungwort. This species now survives only on very old trees or in ancient woods like those at the Hobby Drive. Tree lungwort is a large, green lichen covered with a network of ridges which give it a lung-like appearance, for which

reason it was believed to cure diseases of the lungs. It used to be collected in huge quantities and, unlike its relatives also found in the Hobby Drive, it has so pleasant a smell it was even used in the manufacture of perfume. Today, unfortunately, air pollution has drastically reduced the abundance of lichens so that over-collection could quite rapidly bring some species to the brink of extinction.

By the time the Hobby Drive joins the A39 near Bucks Cross the wind once again prunes the trees and from now on the few small parcels of woodland are confined to the valleys.

Most of the intertidal seashore on this battered coast is narrow and comparatively poor in flora and fauna. Between Hartland Quay and Peppercombe the shore is covered in shifting pebbles, piled into huge ridges by the sea, that grind away both the foot of the cliffs and seashore life alike. South of Hartland Quay and east of Peppercombe the rock platform of the beach widens sufficiently to escape the crushing pebbles of the upper shore. Looking down on these beach platforms from the cliffs you can see the ancient fault-lines criss-crossing the rock and follow the curves of the synclines and anticlines. Where the flat rock platform is low-lying it is patchily covered in brown seaweeds. Saw-wrack and bladder-wrack predominate but several other species are numerous also. On resistant outcrops of rock that stick up above the general shore level can be found black patches of the maritime lichen, *Lichina,* contrasting with the densely-packed white encrustations of barnacles. These wrack-covered shores are the place to search for the purple sandpiper, a small, dark-bodied bird that is an uncommon winter visitor on the North Devon coast. It can often be seen feeding with turnstones among the seaweed-covered rocks below the cliffs of Kipling Tors at Westward Ho! Its dark, purplish-brown colour camouflages it beautifully but the distinctive yellow legs give it away to observant watchers.

Approaching Westward Ho! the rock platform rises considerably. Ebbing tides expose deep clefts in the rocks and leave behind seaweed-fringed rock pools, some wide enough and deep enough to swim in. The rocks disappear abruptly under the sand of Westward Ho! beach and just as abruptly the coast changes from one of ruggedness and storm to one of flatness and shelter.

The Estuary

To an oceanographer an estuary is an inlet where sea water is diluted by fresh water from a river. To a freshwater biologist an estuary is that part of a river which has a variable salt content due to the influence of the sea. The specialists argue the niceties of definition, but the naturalist sees an estuary as a place of great beauty; a wild, often flat land where rivers empty into the sea, where curlews call and wild duck fly. There is another view, held usually by the uninformed, that an estuary is an ugly expanse of useless mud and marsh fit only for reclamation. How wrong they are, for an estuary is where river and sea combine to make unique landscapes with a wealth of wildlife.

The two rivers that jointly form our North Devon estuary are the Taw and the Torridge. Together they drain almost 800 square miles of the North Devon countryside. The Taw rises on Dartmoor while the Torridge rises near Hartland and sweeps round in a great arc to reach the estuary only nine miles from its source. Normally these rivers appear as mere trickles in the huge expanse of the estuary; with a tide that rises and falls as much as 21 feet, the sea is master. At low tide only one and a half square miles of land lies under water, while at high tide over five square miles of land is drowned, and during flood or storm considerably more.

Interestingly, the development of the Taw/Torridge estuary in its present form owes more to the geological forces of the past than to the influence of the rivers and sea of today. Several times, over tens of thousands of years, the sea has swept into what is now our estuary and lapped a shore roughly bounded by the road that runs from Bideford to Barnstaple and on to Saunton. Northam Burrows, Braunton Burrows, Braunton Marsh and Saunton Great Field have lain many times beneath the sea, only to be resurrected in a slightly different form each time the sea has retreated, leaving them high and dry once again. Once, some 300,000 years ago, during the greatest Ice Age of them all, pack ice crowded the shores of North Devon and reached as far as Barnstaple. The 'raised beaches' of Westward Ho! and Saunton, and the submerged forest and kitchen midden on Westward Ho! beach faithfully record some of these rises and falls of sea level as successive Ice Ages came and went.

Raised beaches, as their name suggests, are beaches or seashore formations elevated above present day beaches and obviously beyond the influence of present day seas. At Westward Ho! there is a wave-cut beach platform as much as 25 feet higher than the present seashore. Even more remarkable is the fact that on it, buried in earth, rests a layer of sea-worn pebbles many feet thick – pebbles exactly like those lying at the foot of the cliff 25 feet below. Clearly the pebbles on the raised beach were stranded there many thousands of years ago by a retreating sea and now, as the cliffs erode, they are being exposed once again. At Saunton, beyond the reach of even the highest tides, there are barnacles sandwiched between the grey rock to which they are attached and a massive layer of brown sandstone above. These barnacles are of a *Balanus* species that normally lives at mid-tide level, yet here they sit, higher than the highest tides, left stranded thousands of years ago by a retreating sea. The sandstone that covers them was formed from the sand of a dune-system much larger than the present Braunton Burrows, which in turn succumbed to a newly rising sea.

Perhaps the most fascinating fossil record in the area lies in the submerged forest and associated kitchen midden at Westward Ho! Here there are indications not only of climate, sea level changes and flora and fauna, but also evidence of the activities of man. The submerged forest was first exposed in the winter of 1863/4 by storm seas which had stripped sand and clay off the beach. Some 70 to 80 tree trunks up to 40 feet long, mostly of oak but some of pine or spruce, were discovered embedded in brown peat. They have long since been washed away. With them were an abundance of acorns and hazel nuts, so perfectly preserved that it was in some cases possible to tell from teeth marks and the manner in which the nuts were opened just which small animals had eaten them. During the winter of 1865 the nearby kitchen midden was exposed and soon yielded a wealth of information. A kitchen midden is simply the name for a Stone Age rubbish tip and, taken together with the later discovery of rows of pointed stakes, some in a semi-circle, there was no doubt that this was the site of an encampment: a base from which Stone Age man foraged on the seashore and hunted in the surrounding woodland for game.

The diet of early man, as revealed by the midden, was very varied. Shells of limpets, oysters and mussels were present in large numbers and there were great quantities of crushed bones and bone fragments. Among the species identified from bones were red deer, roe deer, fallow deer, ox, wild boar, wild goat and even wolf. The remains of domestic dog, hedgehog and of man himself – a collar bone – have also been found. The forest and midden are believed to be between 3000 and 6000 years old. From the evidence it seems that the land then was well forested, relatively wet, some distance from the sea (in this location trees would be unable to grow long, straight trunks up to 40 feet high unless a mile or so from the influence of the fierce salt winds) and full of deer and game. However, the presence of a thin layer of recent blue clay above the peat showed that after these dates conditions changed dramatically. This clay was full of shells of the laver spire snail *(Hydrobia)*, a common brackish water species. The peat also contained the seeds of many brackish water plants. Obviously, by this time the sea was rising, destroying the forest and creating within the shelter of the estuary, and probably in the protection of the newly-forming pebble ridge, the flat, salt marsh that was destined to become Northam Burrows.

The pebble ridge that protects Northam Burrows from being swamped by the sea is unique. It is a spit, a massive barrier of grey pebbles 1½ miles long, over 20 feet high and up to 60 feet wide. There are other similar spits on the west coast of England and Wales but only the pebble ridge is composed of cobbles instead of shingle and sand. Almost every visitor who sees the ridge for the first time asks 'How did it get here?' or 'Where do the pebbles come from?' A surprising number find it difficult to believe that it is an entirely natural formation that arose without the intervention of man. The pebbles come from around the north-west coast as far away as Hartland, swept along by the sea in a process known as longshore drifting. Continuous rock falls from the cliffs provide fresh material for the sea to round and roll. Eventually the pebbles reach the ridge, where their progress is slowed but not stopped. Pebbles constantly move along the ridge, finally accumulating on the Greysand spit or dropping into the deep water channel of the estuary.

Westward Ho! as it must have been 6,000 years ago.
Swampy woodlands of oak and pine frequented by wild cattle, wild boar and fallow deer

Pebble Ridge, Westward Ho!

The pebble ridge probably began life as a pebble beach at the foot of a low clay cliff beyond the promontory of Rocks Nose. As the rising sea gradually cut away the cliff the pebbles would finally have stood free on the low-lying land behind, piled by the sea into a huge ridge on the upper shore. Like a giant sausage, the ridge has since been steadily rolled back by the sea; in recent times it has retreated at an average rate of a yard a year. It was this retreat and subsequent erosion of the beach that exposed the submerged forest to view.

Today the pebble ridge is weak and liable to breach and a great deal of effort is spent in trying to stabilise it. Over the centuries the strength and stability of the ridge must have varied, depending on the amount of pebbles reaching it from along the shore. It was undoubtedly stronger in the past due to the delivery of enormous quantities of 'fossil' pebbles released from the raised beach deposits eroded by the sea and from the great jumble of rocks dropped to the shore by the Gore landslip at Bucks Mills. It does seem, however, that whatever man manages to achieve in strengthening the pebble ridge, its eventual fate is sealed. The sea level is still rising and in common with similar structures on our southern shores, Slapton Ley and Chesil Bank for instance, the sea will slowly push back the ridge until it comes to rest at the foot of the hills behind. We might do well to remember the local prophesy: 'When Charles the Third reigns, the sea will reach Bone Hill [Northam Village]'.

Celery-leaved Buttercup   *P. Wakely, Nature Conservancy Council*

Within the protection of the pebble ridge the 650 acres of Northam Burrows sports a well-developed sand-dune system, dune-pasture, salt-marsh and salt pasture. The grazing is relatively good and for centuries the local people have had the right to graze their stock free of any charge. There is also a rubbish tip, started in the 1930s, which has caused incalculable ecological damage to the Burrows. Early phases of tipping were used to create a dam and a road which cut off the sea, making the area less liable to tidal flooding. In consequence, the Burrows is now drier and much more accessible than in the past. One result of this is that many wetland birds that used regularly to breed here are gone. Within living memory, curlew, lapwing and yellow wagtail bred in good numbers, lapwing especially in sufficient numbers for people to collect their eggs for food – an activity which is now illegal, but was then a traditional pastime which, in this case, had little effect on numbers.

Plants were also affected by the changing conditions but many brackish water species found refuge in the extensive system of drainage ditches. Dense clumps of glaucous bulrush grow in the Pill, the main drainage channel, and the celery-leaved buttercup with its peculiar, long-domed head and tiny yellow petals thrives in the muddy ditches. Seeds of both these plants have been recovered from the seashore peat. Celery-leaved buttercup was put to effective, if unusual, use by medieval beggars. Parts of the plant produce angry weals if rubbed into skin abrasions and many beggars used to seek out the plant before entering a village, applying it to their face and hands to make a more convincing case for alms! One plant which as yet shows no sign of decline is the sharp rush. This rare and extraordinary plant grows in dense tussocks up to seven feet high, each of its hundreds of stems tipped with a tough, extremely sharp point. It is the sharpest-leaved plant in Britain and can inflict a painful wound if you chance to walk into one. On Northam Burrows the majority of the rushes grow in a closely crowded colony many acres in extent; a feature, I believe, unique in Britain. A combination of heavy grazing which eliminates its competitors and tough, sharp stems which deter virtually all grazing stock has probably given it the advantage it needs to survive here in such abundance.

Botanically, though, there is nothing here to compare with the vast and spectacular sand-dunes of Braunton Burrows, the 'big brother' to Northam Burrows on the opposite side of the estuary. Indeed, Braunton Burrows is the richest site for wild flowers anywhere in southern England. It is a National Nature Reserve renowned not only for its plants but also for its rare and fascinating insects. The key to the rich diversity of wildlife on Braunton Burrows lies in its variety of habitats. To understand how this variety arose it is worth considering just how the sand-dunes formed and where the sand that makes them came from.

First we must return once more to the time of the Ice Ages. As the ice caps travelled southwards, moving like a slow-flowing river, they ground pieces of rock from the land over which they passed and these were locked into the ice. When the ice reached the area we now know as the Bristol Channel (during successive Ice Ages it was dry land) the slightly warmer climate melted the advancing edge of the ice and the ground-up rock was released – enormous quantities of it over tens of thousands of years. When the climate warmed and the ice retreated the Bristol Channel became flooded once more.

Gradually, the returning sea winnowed out the smaller, harder, granular particles of brown flint and milky-white quartz and transported them as sand towards the shore. Wherever a bay formed some of this sand was thrown on to the beach and where the beach fronted a low, flat expanse of land the wind blew the sand ashore to form sand-dunes. When sand is blown on to a flat surface it tends naturally to form into ripples and the sand-dunes of Braunton Burrows are, in fact, a series of three or four giant ripples much broken and dissected by erosion. The hollows between the ripples lie close to the original bedrock surface and become damp or flooded in the winter. They are known as 'slacks'.

But the story of sand does not end here. If you look at a handful of sand you will also see, besides quartz and flint, small pieces of broken shell, mostly fragments of mussels, cockles and rayed sunset shells, all of which are regularly thrown up on to the beach. These species are all filter-feeders living on bacteria and plankton sieved from seawater, which they constantly circulate over their 'gill-rakers'. In the right conditions they occur in huge numbers, many thousands to the square yard, mussels attaching themselves to rocks, and cockles and rayed sunset shells burying themselves in mud and off-shore sand. Nearly all North Devon's beaches have small pockets composed entirely of broken shells and occasionally deep drifts of shells are washed into bays and on to beaches. This does not necessarily indicate a disaster, just natural mortality among what must be enormous populations, or possibly just large offshore accumulations of shells finally brought to shore by a storm tide. Eventually the shells will all be broken down to become part of the beach sand.

The presence of a high proportion of shell in

Braunton Burrows – Marram Grass and Rushes

the sand of Braunton Burrows is one of the crucial factors contributing to its variety of plant life. Sand composed only of flint and quartz is acid, restricting the range of plants that can grow in it. But sand containing shell can range from very calcareous (limy) to mildly acid as the shell is gradually dissolved away by rain and ground water, thus allowing the growth of a much wider range of plants. Certainly the presence of shell lime can have a marked effect on the growth of marram grass, the most important plant in the evolution of sand-dunes.

Marram grass grows in dense tussocks with roots that run deep into the sand to tap the meagre supplies of water. It can spread rapidly, sending up new plants from its underground rhizomes, but its most remarkable property is its ability to trap and accumulate blowing sand around its thick tussocks. It can happily survive being buried under three feet of sand a year, simply pushing up new shoots as the old leaves are buried. Marram is entirely responsible for the formation of the massive dunes, up to 100 feet high, on Braunton Burrows. Without marram grass sand can only build dunes a few tens of feet in height, and these soon break up. Marram binds the sand, which enables other plants to take root and grow, eventually reducing sand movement almost completely. When that happens, the marram grass begins to die. As well as the loss of moving sand, leaching of lime from the stabilised sand is believed to be one of the major reasons for the die-back of marram.

During the early phases of dune building only water-conserving spiny or succulent plants such as sea holly and sea rocket can survive the arid conditions alongside the marram grass close to the seashore. Sea rocket, with its pretty pink flowers and fleshy leaves, often grows in a thick band between the dunes and the sea, while the sea holly, with its startling blue, domed flowers and grey-blue spiny leaves, grows in clumps scattered about the seaward dunes.

Running among the plants, particularly in the month of May, their mating season, might be found the attractive little wolf spider, *Arctosa perita*. Like many creatures living on sand-dunes, this spider is perfectly camouflaged. Light and dark bands round its legs and a broken, speckled pattern on its body make it almost invisible the moment it stops

Arctosa perita.

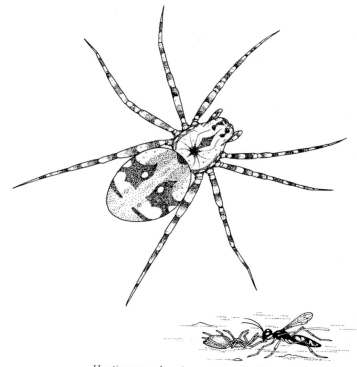

Hunting wasp dragging a paralysed spider to its burrow

Welcombe mouth   L. H. Pratt

Yellow horned poppy. A seaside poppy with the largest seed pods of any British plant   Mike Glover

Fulmar   Mervyn Baker   *Spring Squill   Dennis Heard*

Kingcup   Mike Towns

Spekes Mill Mouth waterfall   Mike Towns

Beard lichens   Mike Towns

Bush Cricket   M. Baker

Sea spleenwort. An unusual fern that grows on sea-sprayed cliffs   Mike Towns

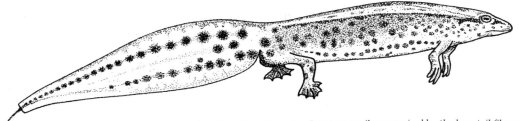

Palmate newt. An amphibian of acid ponds on Braunton Burrows, easily recognised by the long tail filament

moving. Most of the time this spider lives in a silk-lined Y-shaped burrow in the sand. The two arms of the Y emerge at the surface but one is kept permanently closed. In fine weather the spider sits at the open entrance to its burrow, waiting to pounce on passing prey. If disturbed the spider darts back into its burrow, pulling a curtain of web covered in sand grains across the entrance as it disappears inside – another perfect camouflage. The closed entrance to the burrow is used solely as a means of escape from a species of hunting wasp, its most formidable enemy. This wasp detects *Arctosa* burrows with its antennae and tears away the entrance curtain to rush in and attack the spider inside. If lucky, the spider will have time to flee from the closed entrance into the other arm of the Y, ripping aside the protective web to make good its escape. If unlucky, the doomed spider, motionless in fear, puts up no resistance to the wasp and is stung into paralysis and carried off to the wasp's larder. Paralysed, but still living, the spider will be food for larvae hatched from eggs laid on it by the wasp.

Moving inland from the sea, bare patches of sand are thickly colonised by the evening primrose, a tall plant with large, primrose-yellow flowers. During the day the flowers hang limp and shrivelled but as evening approaches they stiffen and open out into a trumpet shape, awaiting pollination by night-flying moths and other insects. In this bare sand animal tracks, too, can be seen. The star-like footprints of voles cluster around marram tussocks and rabbit tracks criss-cross the dunes, while fox prints, one pad firmly in front of the other, run in a straight line. Insect tracks look like the imprints of a minute bicycle tyre, sometimes ending with the dried body of their creator, caught out too long in the sun.

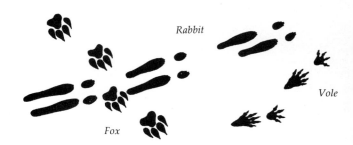

Animal tracks (not to scale)

Further inland stable, grass-covered dunes appear, the short, rabbit-cropped turf speckled with the tiny yellow flowers of dune pansy in spring and the tall, brilliant blue flowering spikes of the viper's bugloss in summer. To see masses of viper's bugloss and evening primrose flowering together is a truly stunning and unforgettable sight. Viper's bugloss is a lime-preferring plant, its name deriving from the similarity of its seeds to a snake's head. Because of this similarity it was believed that the plant was a powerful antidote to snake bite. Other lime-loving plants make their appearance here: the yellow-wort or *blackstonia;* yellow rattle, a plant partially parasitic on grass, with bladder-like seed heads in which the ripe seeds rattle in the wind; the carline thistle with its strangely dried-up appearance; and the rare moonwort fern – all are abundant in the stable dunes.

Mauve sheets of wild thyme carpet these dunes in early summer, the flowers alive with insects seeking nectar from the sweet-scented flowers. Where wild thyme grows, so too will be found ants. Thyme thrives in soil finely worked by ants excavating their galleries and chambers below the surface. One of the most common ants on Braunton Burrows is a small, yellow-brown species less than an eighth of an inch in length, *Lasius alienus* (it has no common English name), which lives in coastal pastures and sandy heaths. Early in the year, as the sun warms the land, the short turf sprouts thousands of miniature 'volcanoes' of sand as the ants dig their tunnels, bringing the sand to the surface through their exit holes grain by grain. In the clammy mists that often shroud the Burrows at this time of year these 'volcanoes' assume weird shapes: surprisingly tall mounds, like miniature termite hills, stuck together with moisture, they collapse when the drying sun breaks through.

Undoubtedly, though, the jewels in the crown of Braunton Burrows are its orchids. June and July are the orchid months, a time when there is a veritable profusion of flowers; richly coloured blossoms in great spikes or delicate clusters. Pyramidal orchid, spotted orchid and fragrant orchid dot the dune turf, but the greatest glory is reserved for the dune slacks, the low-lying troughs between dunes, damp in summer, flooded in winter. Each slack has its own individual flora, depending on the amount of moisture, variability in soil, and size. In wetter slacks marsh helleborine sends up blooms, in patches hundreds strong, from extensive creeping rhizomes. This is probably the most beautiful orchid growing on the Burrows. The large flowers, whitish tinged with purplish-red, hang in loose clusters on long stems. Marsh helleborine seeds are relatively large and can float, enabling the plant to spread easily to new localities. In slightly drier places grow the many varieties of marsh orchid, their colours ranging from a deep pink to the rich magenta of the short dune form. Most varieties have unspotted leaves but some do have spots and one, known as the leopard orchid, has rings on its leaves. The flowering spikes of these orchids can be enormous, reaching up to eighteen inches in height and occasionally sprouting in clusters of three or more on a single plant.

Orchid life histories are exceedingly complicated. They can grow only in association with specific soil fungi, each species of orchid favouring its own particular species of fungus, and they may take many years to germinate. Once germinated it may be as many years again before they flower – seven years between germination and flowering is not uncommon. Pollination is mostly carried out by bees and wasps, the

Winter ice on sharp rush, Northam Burrows   *Mike Towns*

Six-spot Burnet moth. Common in sand-dunes   Mervyn Baker   *Marbled White. An uncommon grassland butterfly   M Glover*

Stinking Iris   Mervyn Baker   *Crab spider   Mike Glover*

Southern Marsh Orchid   *Mervyn Baker*

Common Blue   *Mike Glover*

Clouded Yellow. A migrant butterfly that comes to Britain in large numbers only in hot summers   Mervyn Baker

Marsh Helleborine   P. Wakely, Nature Conservancy Council

sticky pollen-masses or pollinia attaching themselves to the insects' bodies as they enter the flowers in their search for nectar. Other insects commonly involved in pollination are beetles and flies, and one group of orchids, which includes the fragrant orchid, is pollinated by butterflies. Even marvellously camouflaged crab spiders, which hide among the flowers to catch visiting insects, have been seen with pollinia attached to their bodies. The so-called 'insect' group of orchids not only have flowers resembling specific female insects but they also emit a powerful scent which is very attractive to the males of the species they mimic. Pollination takes place not by the insects trying to gather nectar but by the males trying to mate with the imitation female!

Kingcup, or marsh marigold, the round-leaved wintergreen and creeping willow, also make attractive splashes of colour in the slacks. Kingcups, with their large, golden-yellow, buttercup-like flowers occur in only one slack on the whole of the Burrows. Why this should be so is unknown. Their abundance varies from year to year, but they are always a fine sight in the spring. Creeping willow, by contrast, grows wherever the soil is damp enough, covering the ground in dense, low patches or growing as individual plants known affectionately as 'hedgehogs'. Curiously, despite its abundance and its marked changes in colour through the year, the creeping willow is often overlooked. In spring, yellow catkins contrast with the silver of newly-emerging leaves; in autumn the leaves yellow, falling to reveal dark red stems. During summer whole plants may have their leaves reduced to skeletons by the larvae of the poplar beetle. Later, the bright red adults crawl over the willows seeking out mates and places to lay their eggs. If disturbed, these

Water Mint   P. Wakely, Nature Conservancy Council

beetles emit a strong scent of almonds, doubtless to deter predators.

The common water mint is another abundant plant frequently overlooked. It grows in the slacks, kept quite short where rabbits graze, but up to eighteen inches high in the protection of wet ditches. You may miss the summer blooming of its whorls of pinkish-mauve flowers but you can't ignore the pungent aroma of mint released as you casually trample the plant underfoot. Water mint, like garden mint, can be used in mint sauce and has long been regarded as an aid to digestion. Alternatively, you might, like the Arabs, prefer to take it as tea – mindful of its reputation to increase libido! A handful of leaves thrown into your bathwater is very refreshing.

Just as the pebble ridge protects Northam Burrows from the sea so Braunton Burrows provides shelter and protection for Braunton Marsh. Braunton Marsh as we know it today is a relatively recent landscape. Until early in the last century Braunton Marsh and Horsey Island were one huge, continuous salt-marsh, regularly inundated by tidal waters, stretching as far as Braunton Great Field to the north and Wrafton to the east. Because Braunton Marsh had been grazed since time immemorial the more characteristic salt-marsh plants would have been grazed out and replaced by mineral-rich, highly palatable grasses. The most northerly regions of this marsh, least affected by the tide, would have been grasslands of red fescue grass dotted with clumps of mud rush. Nearer the River Taw the red fescue grass would have given way to the more salt-tolerant sea-manna grass and the land would have been dissected by hundreds of drainage gulleys just like those present today at Penhill on the Taw and the Skern at Northam Burrows. The great fertility of this 1200-acre salt-marsh made it an obvious candidate for agricultural reclamation and in 1808 the celebrated agriculturist Vancouver put forward a proposal for reclaiming the marsh from the sea by means of a sea wall. By 1815 the first stage of reclamation was complete. A Great Sea Bank stretched north-east from the present Toll House, following the original channel of the River Caen to Braunton Great Field, stopping short of the marshes at Wrafton and Velator.

Initially, there were calls for Horsey Island to be included within the Great Sea Bank but Vancouver wisely cautioned against this. At that time Horsey Island was the southernmost region of the salt-marsh, still in the early stages of plant colonisation and the mud sticky and infertile. Not until 1854 was the land

Beautiful demoiselle

Mervyn Baker

Watersmeet

Early purple orchid

Mike Tow

Mike Towns

Razorbill   *Mervyn Baker*

Green Hairstreak. Common in the Exmoor valleys
Mervyn Baker

Yew. Rare as a wild plant in North Devon, apparently self-seeded around Woody Bay
Mike Towns

considered fertile enough for reclamation and then a new sea wall was thrown up from the White House on Braunton Burrows to Braunton Pill. Once the Great Sea Bank was constructed Horsey Island was rejuvenated. The drastically changed tidal currents deposited enormous quantities of silt at Horsey Island and salt-marsh plants colonised rapidly, each species succeeded by another as the silt accumulated and the land level slowly rose. The gradual evolution of Horsey Island from 1815 until the construction of the new sea wall in 1854 must have been fascinating. In all likelihood the vegetation was unaffected by grazing at this time because the presence of the Caen river channel at the foot of the Sea Bank would have made access difficult and dangerous.

The vegetation that took hold at Horsey Island was probably not unlike that of the present-day salt-marsh at East-the-Water on the River Torridge. On the East-the-Water salt-marsh the first plant to colonise the sandy mud is *Salicornia*, 'the poor man's asparagus'. This edible, succulent plant grows to a height of about six inches and has an upright, branched, cactus-like appearance. Its shallow roots bind the mud and on the incoming tide its strong stems slow the tidal current and encourage the deposition of more mud. As the depth of the mud increases *Salicornia* gives way to sea-blite and the thick, trailing tufts of the sea-manna grass. This dense mat of foliage traps yet more mud and soon tall-growing plants such as sea aster and sea lavender begin to appear. Beneath them bloom the pink flowers of thrift, equally at home here on the salt-marsh as on the cliffs, and the white flowers of scurvy grass – here *Cochlearia anglica,* a different species from those elsewhere on the coast. At this stage of its formation the salt-marsh fairly buzzes with

Great Sea Bank, Braunton Burrows

Salt Marsh, Bideford East

life. Bumble bees and hover flies flock to the flowers to collect nectar; the michaelmas daisy-like flowers of sea aster are particularly favoured. Beetles are common, feeding on the salt-marsh plants or the creatures that live among them; some species even tunnel in the surface layers of mud, feeding on algae. Spiders too are abundant and one species of wolf spider has altered its behaviour to suit its regularly-flooded habitat. Instead of running away from the advancing water like its relatives, this spider quite deliberately walks down a plant stem into the water, taking refuge among the drowned vegetation. It survives because its hairy body traps a layer of air around it which keeps it well supplied with oxygen until the tide recedes.

Once the salt-marsh at Horsey Island reached this stage it was enclosed. In the process the River Caen was diverted from its outlet beside Braunton Burrows to empty through Braunton Pill. The old channel, choked with reed and willow, is still visible today behind the sea wall.

Freed from the influence of the sea, salt-marshes soon become pastures typical of lowland Britain. Salt is rapidly leached from the soil and the salt-marsh plants gradually disappear, although some species do survive, usually in old saltpans or places where the concentration of salt was particularly high. Mud rush and sea milkweed, for example, can still be found on Braunton Marsh 170 years after enclosure. For wildlife, however, there are new habitats. The extensive system of drainage channels needed to keep the marshes free from flooding provides freshwater habitats unavailable before. The ditches support a wealth of marsh and water plants including water plantain and branched bur reed. Otters still play and hunt among the reeds, and brilliantly coloured dragonflies dart

Drainage Channel, Braunton Burrows

back and forth along the ditches. Unfortunately, modern ditch-dredging methods have caused the loss of many rare plants such as bladderwort and fen sedge and now herbicides are a new and potent threat to those that remain. The bladderwort is an extraordinary, carnivorous plant that captures and digests water fleas. Each of the many bladders on its stems has a hair-trigger, which if set off by a passing water flea, throws open the bladder and sucks in the hapless water flea. On the bankside grow clumps of yellow flag with their short-lived yellow 'fleur-de-lys' flowers, while careful searching might reveal lesser skullcap and marsh speedwell. The ungrazed sea wall of Horsey Island is also botanically rewarding. The more spectacular species are found on the seaward side above the mean tide level. Here can be found specimens of the yellow horned poppy, with the longest seed pods of any British plant, and

Scurvey Grass   Marsh Samphire   Sea Aster

The greatest concentration of birds, though, occurs in the estuary proper, feeding on the teeming life that thrives in the apparently infertile mud. The Taw/Torridge estuary is of national and regional importance for wintering wildfowl and waders. It supports more than one per cent of the total British population of birds such as oystercatcher, golden plover, ringed plover, sanderling and curlew and regionally the estuary is important for wigeon, shelduck, lapwing and redshank. The sheer number of birds is astonishing. During the midwinter peak there may be more than 15,000 birds in the estuary, all of them supported by the salt-marshes and the millions of burrowing and crawling creatures that live in the bare expanses of mud.

Among these are *Corophium*, barely an eighth of an inch long, which live in shallow, U-shaped burrows and can occur in thousands to the square yard. These are a favourite food of redshanks which may eat them at the prodigious rate of one a second! Laver spire snails, which are equally abundant, are food for both small waders such as dunlin and ringed plover and larger birds such as shelduck. At first it seems impossible that so big a bird as a shelduck can live on such tiny snails: its trick is to sieve the snails from soft mud with its beak by sweeping its head from side to side in a wide arc until it has a good mouthful. Larger mud-dwelling animals and those that burrow deeper, such as ragworm and lugworm, fall prey to long-billed curlews and godwits, although the smaller waders can catch them as they move up their burrows to meet the incoming tide. Ringed plover sometimes carry captured ragworms to a nearby pool and wash them before eating them. But not everything is in the birds' favour; lugworms at least have

in some years there are stunning silver sheets of the delicate and aromatic sea wormwood.

The wide, open plains of the Braunton marshes and to a lesser extent the open pasture of Northam Burrows support large, mixed flocks of wintering lapwing and golden plover. These birds prefer old, established permanent grasslands with their diverse insect prey. The Golden plover are nervous birds and any disturbance sends the flock into the air, sometimes many thousands strong. From a distance the flock looks like animated smoke, disappearing in a flash of silver as they turn to show their bright white undersides, reappearing as they turn again to show their dark backs. In wetter parts of the marshes snipe probe for earthworms with their long bills. These have a sensitive, flexible tip with which they are able to detect the worm in its burrow and deftly grasp it without the need for the whole beak to be opened.

learned to fight back. Often their U-shaped burrows are too deep even for curlews to reach them so the birds wait for the lugworms to ascend their shafts to defecate before striking. At this point, with speed, the lugworm can escape by detaching its tail, just like a lizard, leaving the bird with just a wriggling appendage while the worm retreats to the safety of its burrow. Thick-shelled mud-dwellers like cockles are not immune to attack either. The black and white oystercatcher uses his long red bill not only to probe for ragworms in mud and earthworms in pasture, but also to hammer open cockles to get to the nourishing flesh inside.

The best place in the estuary to watch waders and wildfowl is the Skern at Northam Burrows. A road runs beside the mudflat and the birdwatcher can observe from the comfort of the car. On incoming tides the birds are pushed slowly towards the road, affording the watcher close and entertaining views. Brent geese and wigeon can be seen feeding avidly on weed floated up by the tide and at the waterline many different waders patter about searching for food. During spring and autumn passage the regular waders are joined by rarities such as little stint, curlew sandpiper and grey phalarope. Terns are also frequent then, the commonest visitor being the sandwich tern, but arctic tern, common tern and little tern are seen regularly. Landward, Greysand Lake and Goosey Pool attract teal and shoveller, two beautiful ducks that sieve food from the water margins. These seasonal lakes are also daytime roosts for the hundreds of gulls attracted to Northam Burrows by the lure of easy food on the nearby rubbish tip. Black headed and herring gull are by far the commonest but in winter they are joined by greater and lesser black-backed and common gull. Occasionally exciting rarities such as glaucous gull and little gull come in from the sea.

Some other good birdwatching spots on the estuary are Instow Sands, where a number of rare species have been seen, Fremington Pill, where spotted redshank overwinter each year and from the disused railway at Heanton Court. The outer estuary between Northam Burrows and Braunton Burrows is good for sea-watching. Rafts of eider duck are regular in winter and gannets plunge-dive for fish off the bar in the summer. On the seashore, turnstones pick among the pebbles and rocks and sanderling rush to and fro like small clockwork toys among the waves.

Oystercatchers roosting at high tide

Morte Slates

Saunton to Ilfracombe

Woolacombe Sands

From Saunton to Exmoor the coast is dramatic but gentle. Rolling hills and a milder climate contrast with the flat, wind-blasted uplands around Hartland. Resistant rocks jut out to sea in prominent headlands enclosing golden beaches and billowing sand-dunes. The rocks that form this coast outcrop in horizontal layers, progressing from multi-coloured sand-stones in the south to shiny grey slates in the north. On the shore the sea-rounded pebbles so characteristic of the Hartland coast are gone and instead massive rocks are piled below the cliffs, or fine, silty deposits of grey slate collect in small embayments.

Around Saunton Down and Baggy Point there is a series of raised beaches and a number of geological curiosities from the intensely cold periods of the Ice Ages. On the Croyde Bay side of Baggy Point several deep 'ice-wedges' can be seen in the cliffs. These are cracks caused by the seasonal freezing and thawing of the ground during a period when North Devon was an area of permafrost tundra, like northern Canada or Siberia. In winter the terrible cold cracked the ground, and in the brief summer meltwater from the partial thaw trickled into the cracks, only to be refrozen when winter returned. Year after year the freezing water expanded, forcing the cracks ever wider and deeper. At Saunton there are the remains of another strange permafrost feature – deep, circular pits in the sandstone which often reach down to the bedrock of the modern shore. Inside these 'pipes', unless breached by recent erosion, is loose sand. Here, it seems, during the period of freeze and thaw, meltwater percolated

Saunton Sands and Braunton Burrows

through the sandstone dissolving away the lime cement (provided by the sea shells in the original sand) that holds the sandstone together. This left a pipe in the sandstone partially filled with grains of flint and quartz, the original mineral composition of the sand that built the sandstone rock.

Below the cliffs of Saunton and Baggy, above the reach of normal tides, there are numerous 'erratics' – large and small boulders of rock types unknown in Devon or indeed in southern England. These boulders are mostly of granites or quartz which occur only in western Scotland or north-west England. The boulders must have been transported to our North Devon shores by ice – probably the same pack-ice which crowded into the estuary 300,000 years ago. In between the periods of numbing cold there were long spells of warmth, with at times a climate much warmer than today's. Among fossil shells

discovered in the cliffs at Saunton were those of a warm-water cockle found today no further north than Falmouth in south Cornwall.

Although not as warm now as it was in the distant past, the south-facing cliffs along this coast can become very hot. Perhaps because of this, at Saunton, Baggy Point and Woolacombe a number of garden plants have become naturalised on the cliffs and grow happily and profusely among the native flora. At Saunton and Baggy dark green patches of Hottentot fig *(Mysembryanthemum)* cascade down the cliffs, brilliant with big daisy-like flowers in summer, and at Woolacombe silver clumps of *Cinerarea* (silver ragwort) grow in abundance around Cobesgate beach. The warmth and rich soils of Saunton also encourage wallflowers and the sea heath, a native plant usually found on southern and eastern coasts of Britain. It is strange to find it here, but this too is planted in gardens, so it may be another escape. True natives, though, are the rare sea stock and the handsome stinking iris. Sea stock with its soft, felted, silvery leaves and pink stock-like flowers grows only in a few scattered localities in North Devon and South Wales. Stinking iris, on the other hand, is widely distributed and often pops up in the most unlikely places. On the cliffs it is more likely to be noticed for its long-lasting orange berries rather than its dark green, sword-like leaves or its quite beautiful but short-lived purplish flowers. 'Stinking' refers to the smell given off when the leaves are crushed, a smell some find unpleasant but which has also earned this iris the name 'roast beef plant'.

Some other plants, apparently totally out of place, grow on the shore below Saunton Down. In isolated pockets there are what must be the smallest salt-marshes in Devon; patches of soil only a few yards square have fallen from the cliffs and been colonised by salt-marsh plants. They are just within range of storm tides but are also fed by freshwater springs from the cliff. Mud rush, cord grass, sea-manna grass, sea lavender and sea plantain all occur in these extraordinary miniature marshes.

Above the cliffs of Saunton runs the B3231, a stretch of road with some of the most magnificent views in North Devon. Framed in spring by the tall, yellow-flowering umbels of alexanders, the thoughtfully provided lay-bys at the side of this road offer an unequalled panorama over Bideford Bay. Lines of breaking waves surge on to Saunton Sands; the dunes of Braunton Burrows seem to march on endlessly – an alien, broken and treeless landscape. Travelling further on and rounding the headland the road comes suddenly and breathtakingly into Croyde

Baggy Point across Croyde Bay

Bay. On a bright summer's day the water is a deep blue, with white, foaming breakers rolling noisily on to the shore; but whatever the weather, this is a most charming little bay.

Behind the sands of Croyde beach lies a cluster of sandhills and like all dune systems in North Devon, they are suffering severe erosion. Each year the sea nibbles away at the face of the dunes but, more importantly, it is increased public pressure that has caused the most damage. Unrestricted public access has destroyed the protective cover of vegetation and caused sand to blow away, leaving ugly chasms in the hills. Sand smoking out of a breached dune in a gale force wind is an awesome sight and being unfortunate enough to be caught in such a sandstorm is to experience a stinging, maddening bombardment. Eyes, ears and mouth fill with sand and your only desire is to escape from the storm. At Croyde, Woolacombe and Northam Burrows the problem of sand erosion is so great that large areas of the dunes have been closed to the public. Sand-fences have been erected to catch sand, and marram grass – that marvellous pioneer – has been extensively planted. But it takes many years to halt dune erosion and even if successful all the painstaking work can be destroyed by a carelessly-dropped cigarette in a summer drought.

From Croyde there is a footpath that runs right round Baggy Point to Woolacombe sands. It must surely be one of the most exhilarating walks on the North Devon coast. High up on the breezy headland the path looks first across the wide open expanse of Bideford Bay to where on clear days the mysterious island of Lundy looms on the horizon, only to disappear once more in summer haze or driving winter rain. Rounding the point the view is northward towards the long, golden

Morte Slates

beach of Woolacombe, with Morte Point in the distance.

Hottentot fig, thrift, sea campion, kidney vetch and rock samphire all grow on the cliffsides here. Rock samphire, with its succulent leaves and sulphur-yellow flowers, grows on every ledge and crevice where it can gain a hold. Most of us pass it by without a second glance, but not so very long ago it was eagerly sought after and sold by street traders under the name of 'crest marine'. Pickled, it was considered a delicacy and gatherers would risk their lives to collect it from the crumbling cliffs where it prefers to grow. Even in Shakespeare's time collecting samphire was regarded as a dangerous occupation and was referred to in *King Lear*:

Half-way down hangs one that
gathers samphire; dreadful trade!

Before striding out on to the clift-top path look for the lichen-covered whale bones beside the path. They are all that remains of a whale beached at Croyde in 1915. The bones were moved to the cliffs by the Hyde family of Baggy House to prevent their destruction by vandals. Further on, just before the National Trust gate, there is a scrubby patch of trees and bushes.

Inside the ring of wind-clipped trees is a small marshy area and a trickling stream where once there was a pond. Great willow herb now grows thickly in the mud and the beautiful pink flowers of pink purslane sparkle beneath the trees in summer. This delightful spot is a haven for migrating songbirds. Each spring and autumn thousands fly past the headland and some always seek out this place for shelter, rest and to drink from the stream. Finches, larks, pipits and warblers pass through and sometimes a spotted flycatcher can be seen darting out from its perch to catch a passing insect.

There are birds to be seen around the cliffs too; sea-going birds with little allegiance to the land except as a place to rest or nest. At the foot of the sheer slabs of lichen-encrusted rock of Baggy Point itself shags rest on the reefs and spread their wings to dry. These are relatives of the perhaps more familiar cormorant but they are smaller and have a shimmering, greenish sheen to their feathers. For generations they have nested on these inaccessible rocks with oystercatchers and gulls as their companions. Further from the shore sea ducks may be seen bobbing up and down on the waves, perfectly at home in even the roughest seas. Common scoter and eider are regularly seen in small 'rafts', occasionally diving deep for shellfish attached to offshore rocks. These ducks will dive to a depth of 20 feet or more and stay submerged for a relatively long time. The eider has a strong, rasping bill eminently suited to tearing sea anemones or mussels from the underwater rocks. Male eider sport a gorgeous plumage of black and white with a flush of pink on the breast and green on the head. Common scoter males by contrast have only a bright yellow patch on their beaks to relieve their all-black plumage. The females of both ducks are a drab brown as befits birds which incubate their eggs in open sites with no camouflage other than their own colouring to protect them. It is from eider ducks that we get eiderdown – the feathers the incubating bird uses to line its nest and protect its eggs and young from the freezing temperatures of its northern breeding range.

Northward around Baggy Point the descending footpath leads to Putsborough sands and a completely different landscape. Behind are the rocky ramparts of the Point while ahead is the great golden sweep of

Rock Samphire   *P. Wakely, Nature Conservancy Council*

Woolacombe sands. On the northern side of Baggy Point the rocks change from massive grey sandstones to the multi-coloured layers of the Upcott Slates. In the cliffs the coloured rocks are in wide bands one above the other but the colours are obscured by an enormous abundance of lichens and barnacles which impart their own colour to the rocks. The true, startlingly bright colours of these slates are only revealed in the attractive jumble of purple, green and grey boulders at the foot of the cliff.

Growing at the highest level above the sea, up as far as the rocks and stone walls at the top of Baggy Point, is *Ramalina,* the sea ivory. This small, pale-green lichen grows in tufts on every outcrop of rock. In the Shetlands, sheep survive the harsh conditions by subsisting on this lichen when times are hard – quite extraordinary considering that mainland sheep have never been known to eat it. Lower down the cliffs, within the reach of drenching sea spray, grow the orange patches of the lichen *Caloplaca* and below this, where the sea crashes and foams on the highest tides, is a wide black band of *Verrucaria.* So thin is this lichen and so closely is it pressed to the rocks, that it is often mistaken for part of the rock itself or taken for large patches of dried oil. At Baggy it obscures the natural purple-red colour of the slate just as thick, grey encrustations of barnacles obscure the sea-green of the rocks lower down. The division between the black band of lichen and the grey of the barnacles is abrupt and is known as the 'barnacle line'. It seems that on nearly vertical rocky shores like these conditions can change so drastically that within even a range of a few inches it becomes impossible for the barnacles to survive. The barnacle line can be traced round most of Baggy Point and Morte Point. Other marine life is sparse, confined mainly to limpets and top shells. There are few seaweeds, though occasionally, when the tide is very low, there may be glimpses of dense beds of tangle, their fringed fronds drooping from thick stems anchored to offshore rocks.

The acres of sand on Woolacombe beach show few signs of life, but life there is in abundance. Most of it lives off shore or buried deep in the protective sand low down on the beach. Searching for shells and cast-up plants and animals is the best way of finding out about the denizens of sandy shores. Shells are thrown up, sometimes in prodigious quantities, by the 'ground-sea' – a local term for the noisy, churning type of swell that drags debris from the sea bottom and moves it to the shore. Other, less common, creatures appear on the beach at roughly the same time every year, usually exhausted or dying, after breeding or laying eggs in the intertidal zone.

Razor shells, named after their resemblance to the old-fashioned cut-throat razor, are the largest molluscs found on our North Devon shores. Their empty shells are common on the beaches but trying to find a live one is an almost impossible task. They can be seen only on the lowest of tides with part of the shell protruding from the sand. Within seconds, at the slightest hint of a footfall or shadow, they can pull the entire length of their shells deep into the sand by means of their muscular, digging foot. The large, spiral shells of the common whelk, a scavenger on dead and decaying sea creatures, are also commonly

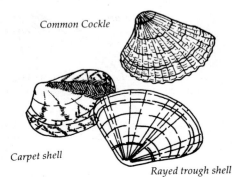

Common Cockle

Carpet shell

Rayed trough shell

washed up on these sandy shores. Most are empty, but some may contain a hermit crab which blocks the entrance of the shell with its large claw to protect its soft, vulnerable body within. Many of the bivalve shells washed ashore, such as venus cockles and sunset shells, are found to have a tiny, neat hole drilled in their apex. This is made by the predatory necklace shell, a large, brown-shelled mollusc that pushes its way through underwater sand searching for prey. When it encounters a bivalve it extends its body as a smothering mantle around the luckless shell and drills a hole into it, aided by the secretion of acid which softens the shell. Once through the shell the drill pierces muscle, weakening the bivalve, and forcing it to open to be consumed by the necklace shell.

In early summer a number of exotic creatures appear on the sandy beaches, among them the masked crab, sea-mouse and sea-hare. The masked crab, so called because of the face-like mask on its carapace, is usually washed up dead. Most specimens are male, easily recognised by their ridiculously long claws – twice the length of their bodies. Normally these light-brown crabs lie buried in sand with their long, bristly antennae extended like a tube to circulate oxygenated water to their gills. The sea-mouse too lives buried in sand but it is often washed up by storms. It resembles a slug, is about 6 inches long and 2 inches wide and is covered in iridescent spines. This creature is actually a worm; but so unlike a worm is it, and so beautiful the armour of spines, shining with all the colours of the rainbow, that zoologists have given it the Latin name *Aphrodite*, after the Greek goddess of beauty. To find the sea-hare means a search among the rocks around Barricane beach at the north end of Woolacombe sands. This olive-green or brown animal is much more slug-like than the sea-mouse and comes to lay salmon-pink strings of eggs among the rocks and weeds of the shore. Out of the water it is a shapeless mass, but when returned to its natural habitat its billowing, rippling mantle gives it an unexpected grace.

From Barricane beach the shore is predominantly rocky again and there is yet another change in rock type, this time to the Morte and Ilfracombe slates. Deposited in

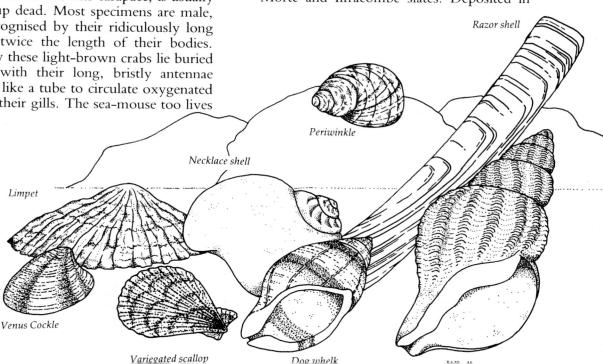

Razor shell

Periwinkle

Necklace shell

Limpet

Venus Cockle

Variegated scallop

Dog whelk

Morte Point

shallow seas as fine sediments from a land mass that lay roughly in the position of present-day Wales, these slates, like all of North Devon's rocks, have been subjected to great pressures and intense heat. During these upheavals the milky-white quartz in the rock melted and forced its way into cracks and weaknesses. These veins now stand out conspicuously on the shore, more resistant to erosion than are the soft slates. One very thick band, blushed with a delicate pink, towers above the shore on Combesgate beach. The Morte slate itself reflects sunlight with an almost blinding intensity. It is soft, smooth and silver-grey, with a unique satin-like quality. The rock layers stand almost upright, great slabs in the cliffs; with broken, jagged reefs along the shore projecting like dragons' teeth. The humped appearance of Morte Point is due to the presence of two harder bands of rock among the many layers. After

Morte Point the coast loses the great embayments and jutting promontories, instead breaking up into a series of charming coves and secluded bays. All along the north-facing coast the beaches are covered by innumerable tiny, ground-down fragments of grey slate, shining silver around Morte Point and gradually becoming darker towards Ilfracombe. At Watermouth, near Combe Martin, the bay is one of the best examples in North devon of a drowned river valley. The sea has cut, and still continues to cut, a wide swathe inland along the course of the river, creating an unusual sheltered bay.

Grasslands dominate this coastal region of soft grey slate. Drifts of bluebells grow in neglected, ungrazed places and violets, celandines and primroses compete for a space in the grass. But in spring gorse is the glory of the cliffs. Whole hillsides turn yellow with blossom. Gorse flowers hum with visiting

Twayblade   P. Wakely, Nature Conservancy Council

permanent pasture is ploughed up and reseeded. Semi-wild places such as these on the coast are often the last refuge for creatures ousted by the onslaught of modern farming methods. On top of the anthills there may be collections of dung pellets left by rabbits who use the hills as convenient look-out posts and territorial boundary markers. More often than not there will also be a fox dropping nearby: grey, full of fur – quite likely that of a rabbit, and small bones and feathers.

Hedgerows, with their complement of songbirds such as whitethroats and yellowhammers, are frequent in the rolling countryside around the coast, but woodlands are rare. The only woodland of any appreciable size is that of the Borough Valley at Lee. Much of this has, unfortunately, been sacrificed to the ubiquitous and sterile conifer, though thankfully most of the broadleaved woodland that remains is in the more sensitive landscape areas open to public view. At Lee, an arm of the woodland swings up the valley and beneath the tall oaks is a dense understorey of rhododendron. Regarded as a forest 'weed' because of its vigorous,

Watermouth

bees and brightly coloured stonechats perch on prominent branches to deliver their chattering song. Late summer brings the dark green fritillary butterfly, winging powerfully along the hillsides defying the wind in search of violets on which to lay eggs. Moles throw up heaps of earth in furious activity and voles tunnel in thick grass or beneath the surface of the soil. Wherever the land remains undisturbed by tractor or plough there are clusters of mounds of the yellow meadow ant. Each of these humps of finely tilthed earth has grown up over many years as the ants have painstakingly brought up the soil from below. Meadow ant mounds are becoming increasingly rare in the countryside as smothering growth the rhododendron nevertheless makes a marvellous splash of purple on the valleyside in early summer. In clear spaces grow the long, green, inconspicuous spikes of the twayblade orchid and the straggling stems of sweet woodruff. Woodruff gives off an evocative scent of hay when dried. Used in the traditional manner, interleaved between linen in the airing cupboard, it brings a fresh scent of summer to bedding and clothing.

The Lee valley is quite beautiful, and an unexpected contrast to the rest of the coast. Known as 'the valley of the fuschias' Lee valley has a haunting atmosphere that draws people to it time and again. The fuschias are no longer as abundant as they were but efforts are being made to replant and restore some of the former glory. Spring mornings often begin with a dense, blanketing mist that creeps up the valley from the sea bringing an unnatural quiet and a damp chill. Yet at the top of the valley the sun will be shining down on the swirling, billowing mists below. The valley terminates in a small, rocky bay and there is always a strand line of rotting seaweed at the foot of the sea wall. Masses of tangle and sea belt torn from the rocks by stormy seas mingle with thousands of limpet shells, yellow, brown and red flat periwinkle shells and pieces of pink quartz.

The most famous region of foreshore on the northern coast of Devon is that of Ilfracombe. It was at this populous seaside watering hole that the great Victorian naturalist Gosse explored the seashore, studying and classifying its inhabitants. Charles Kingsley, the Victorian author North Devon considers its own, spent many hours exploring this shore too. In his time he was as well known a naturalist as he was a writer of novels. The attraction of Ilfracombe to the

Lee Bay

Rock Pools at Ilfracombe

seashore naturalist lies not only in its deep harbour, rocky shore and rock pools but also in its wealth of warm–water species encouraged by the benign south–western climate.

Like all rocky shores, that of Ilfracombe can be divided into zones. These zones are based on the amount of time the many species of plants and animals have to spend out of water exposed to wind, sun and rain. On the upper shore plants and animals may wait days or weeks for the sea to reach them while the middle shore is covered and uncovered on every tide. The lower shore is only briefly exposed by an ebbing tide and has some similarity to the sub-littoral zone, a region just off shore and permanently submerged beneath the sea. Highest on the upper shore is the 'splash zone' where only salt spray washes the rocks. Animals that live in this zone are almost fully terrestrial but still dependent on the sea for dispersal of young or for its protective cloak of dampness and humidity. The small periwinkle and sea slater, a maritime woodlouse, crowd into rock crevices, emerging at night to feed. Small periwinkles are herbivorous, feeding on lichens, while the scuttling sea slater is a scavenger, searching the shore for plant or animal remains. Sea slaters are so strictly nocturnal that even strong moonlight is enough to keep them hidden in their rocky retreats. Lower down, provided the scour of sea and loose boulders is not too great, there is a band of seaweed across the rock; channelled wrack above and flat or spiralled wrack below. These seaweeds can withstand the harsh conditions of the upper shore, remaining uncovered by the sea perhaps for days on end. Channelled wrack especially becomes dry and brittle, losing as much as 70 per cent of its water, yet it survives until revived by the next high tide. The channels on the underside of its fronds, which close up as it dries, conserve just enough precious water to keep it alive.

Around and below the seaweeds are the white encrustations of barnacles and black patches of mussels. Barnacles thrive where the sea crashes over the rocks but mussels, held fast to the rock by a series of anchoring 'byssus' threads, prefer sites with more shelter from the pounding waves. Among them and over them, feeding on them by drilling through their armour of shell with a specially modified tongue, are dog whelks. Interestingly, the colour of dog whelk shells is influenced by the prey they eat. Specimens feeding on barnacles are white and those feeding on mussels are dark, while those which alternate their feeding between barnacles and mussels are striped black and white! Dog whelks lay their eggs in small, straw-coloured capsules stuck in clusters to rocks. Each capsule contains a hundred or more eggs but only half a dozen or so are fertile. The infertile eggs serve as food for the newly-hatched young while they are still in the capsule. Towards the middle of the shore limpets appear, stuck fast to the rock by a powerful suction and adhesive force. With them are the common periwinkle and thick top-shell. All of them are grazers, scraping the thin film of algae off the rocks as they glide slowly over them. Limpets feed in a very limited home range and after feeding always return to exactly the same spot. Their distinctive 'chinaman's hat' shape and strong adhesive grip defy the full force of the surging waves. So tightly do they press to the surface on soft rocks that their 'wiggling' action, as they settle into their 'home' spot, wears a pit into the rock face. If the rock is hard it is their own shells that wear to fit the rock, so when they return from feeding they must orientate themselves precisely to the outline of the rock to obtain the maximum grip. Periwinkles and top shells make no attempt to fight the waves. Instead they have rounded shells and avoid damage by simply letting the waves take them and roll them harmlessly about the shore.

Scattered about the middle and lower shore, on rock ledges, under overhangs and in deep clefts are those gardens of delight, the rock pools, the most exacting of all habitats on the shore. Where the sea rises and falls with unchanging regularity life has only to protect itself temporarily against the drying sun, wind or cold and wait for the tide to return. But in a rock pool conditions can vary from one extreme to another in the course of a single tide. Rain can quickly dilute the seawater in a pool so that it becomes almost fresh. On the other hand, dageen is also known as Irish moss and is the famous edible seaweed used in the preparation of alginate jelly. Deeper pools lower down on the shore where conditions are more stable support several seaweeds that are normally found only off shore. At Ilfracombe tangles and sea belt fringe the edges of the pools and forests of pod seaweed flourish in the deep water.

A search among the fronds of tangles or sea belt might reveal the blue-rayed limpet, a beautiful, glossy, smooth-shelled limpet up to an inch long with electric-blue spots radiating in lines along the shell. Under the protective fronds of any of the seaweeds crabs can always be found; the brick-red edible crab is an uncommon visitor but the shore crab is found everywhere, seeking shelter under stones as well as under the seaweed. This brown and green crab resents being handled. If it is backed into a corner it stands on tiptoe and spreads its claws wide in a characteristic menacing gesture, though it seldom gives a painful nip. A similar crab, more often seen in flooded gulleys, is the velvet swimming crab or fiddler crab. It has paddle-shaped hind legs, swims rather than runs and is covered in short, dense, brown fur. Like so many other sea creatures, it has brilliant blue lines on its body; in this crab along the edges of its shell. Fishes, too, hide in the weed but if flushed out will frantically dart about then suddenly stop and remain quite still, relying on their camouflaging colouring to protect them. Rock gobies and the common blenny, or shanny, are abundant in rock pools. The shanny is so well adapted to its intertidal existence that it is said to leave the water to sunbathe! It certainly spends a lot of time out of water, laid up in cracks in the rocks. There is nothing more unnerving when searching through hanging curtains of seaweed or green or orange sponge-encrusted rocks than to be suddenly confronted by a cold fish eye watching you from a dark crevice.

Camouflage on the seashore is not only achieved through body colouring. The small sea urchin *(Psammechinus miliaris)* actively covers itself in bits of weed and shell to disguise itself from predators. Like all sea urchins, it feeds on small animals and eats some vegetation. It moves slowly about the bottom of pools and can climb up the sides of rocks. The bodies of sea urchins are covered in sharp spines but these are not used for walking. Close examination will reveal hundreds of long, thin, transparent tube-feet that are extremely strong and have a powerful suction grip. These are used not only for transport but also to grasp and tear at prey.

Rock pools, whether shallow or deep, also harbour those most fascinating and beautiful of all sea-shore creatures, the sea anemones. Ilfracombe is particularly fortunate in having a good complement of sea anemones and some of the more exotic species were first discovered there. Commonest, occurring all over the middle and lower shore, is the beadlet anemone. Out of water it is a shiny blob of red jelly; in water, its tentacles open out like the petals on a flower – but petals of a deadly intent. All anemones are carnivorous, eating small water animals, and even small fish, that stray within the range of their tentacles. Prey is fired on with stinging, paralysing threads and drawn into the central gullet by the ring of tentacles.

Largest of the anemones, up to 4 inches across, is the dahlia anemone, found in pools on the lower shore. Its multi-coloured column is sticky and usually has pieces of shell and gravel adhering to it, making it very difficult to spot. Smallest of the anemones are *Sagartia,* as little as half an inch across, which can be found low down on the shore under overhangs and in cracks in the bottom of pools. The colours of these beautiful anemones are extremely varied and defy description. Tentacles may be white or pink on a deep orange or multi-coloured column, or various shades of brown or cream, radiating out in a pattern of concentric rings from the centre. Beautiful though *Sagartia* may be, the most stunning of all the anemones must be the plumose anemone. Normally a sub-littoral species, it can occasionally be found in deep pools on the lower shore or on pier piles. Unlike the other anemones its tentacles are very fine and very numerous, crowning the long, slimy column in a white or pinkish-brown feathery mass.

Normally anemones are able to withdraw their tentacles into their columns but one western species, the snakelocks anemone, is unable to do so. This green or brown mid-shore species is quite common on the Ilfracombe foreshore in sheltered, sunny pools, embedded deep in cracks with only its constantly waving tentacles exposed. Its preference for sunny pools and its inability to withdraw its tentacles has evolved in response to the presence of millions of minute single-celled algae living in its tissues. The algae need to be in daylight as much as possible to survive and they probably benefit from being protected within the anemone's body, while the anemone benefits by the algae removing waste products from its body. There is yet another curious thing about this anemone; in response to a finger being drawn through its tentacles the snakelocks anemone will fire hundreds of invisible stinging threads – they are, of course, harmless to humans! If there was ever any doubt about the ability of these creatures to ensnare and capture vigorous prey like small fish, the surprisingly strong pull of these threads will dispel it.

Finally, mention must be made of the cup corals. Anemones are closely related to the reef-building corals of the tropics and two solitary corals occur in Britain. The Devonshire cup coral and the scarlet and gold star coral are both confined to south-western coasts where they are very rare and local, the scarlet and gold star coral particularly so. How marvellous then that this coral was first discovered by Gosse in 1852 in a rock pool at Ilfracombe. This is his description:

The new species may be at once recognised by its brilliant colours. The whole of the body and disc, exclusive of tentacles, is of a rich orange, yellower in younger specimens, almost approaching scarlet in adults, especially when contracted, for distension not only pales the hue, but causes the yellow element to be more apparent. The tentacles, about fifty in number, in my largest specimens, are of a fine gamboge yellow. The royal colours in which the present species is arranged – scarlet and gold – suggest the specific name of *regia*.

The corals are not at first easily distinguishable from ordinary sea anemones but when the tentacles are contracted and the body withdrawn, the limy skeleton, about half an inch long, is readily apparent. They are only found at the lowest levels of the shore and then usually only on the lowest tides.

Heddon's Mouth

Exmoor Coast

Hangman's Hill, Combe Martin

The beauty and glory of Exmoor owes as much to its majestic coastline as it does to its bleak upland moors, green fields and famous beech hedges. To many visitors Exmoor **is** the coast, and the sea is certainly the foil for much of its most breathtaking scenery. Towering cliffs, many almost a thousand feet high, march from Combe Martin to the flatlands of Bridgwater Bay in Somerset. There are no reefs off these cliffs and no jutting headlands to defy the waves and shelter sand-filled bays. Instead, the sea has carved back the land leaving a 'roller-coaster' chain of massive hog's-back cliffs that plummet to unreachable rocky shores.

Exmoor, unlike Dartmoor, Devon's other national park, is not formed from granite. Its coastal cliffs and high, rounded uplands are composed of hard, resistant sandstones and grits. In the steep valleys and on the plunging cliffs these hard rocks weather into great fields of broken, angular stone. This is scree, enormous quantities of rock fragments flaked from prominent crags by summer sun and winter frost which move imperceptibly but relentlessly down the great grey slopes. The depth of stone and the mobility of the scree prevents the accumulation of soil and the establishment of plants. Where the covering of stone is thin an occasional tree gains a hold but, stunted by the wind and deformed by the ever-moving scree these appear to be crawling up the slopes like malignant growths.

Ice Age scree formation was responsible for the characteristic hog's-back shape of Exmoor's sea cliffs. Intense cold and deeply penetrating frosts shattered stone from exposed crags, eroding the rock upward in a gently curving arc. Hidden beneath the rapidly forming scree the newly-shaped bedrock was protected from further erosion, to be revealed only when a warmer climate brought the rise in sea level that swept the scree away. At Heddon Valley and Foreland Point the still-active scree slopes are hundreds of feet high, while at the Valley of the Rocks at Lynton erosion is less vigorous and the slopes less spectacular. Here, though, the exposed crags have weathered into strange pinnacles of rock topped with huge, occasionally precariously perched, boulders. This wide, flat valley is dry. No stream runs here today, yet the valley was obviously carved by water. It seems that Ice Age coastal streams were blocked by ice and debris which forced them to run parallel with the shore before finding their outlets. Flat cliff-top terraces at Lee Bay (Lynton) and Woody Bay mark the course of these extinct streams from the Valley of the Rocks. A similar and more clearly defined prehistoric valley can also be traced along the coast from Hartland to Speke's Mill Mouth.

Migrating scree eventually falls to the seashore or is transported seaward by swiftly flowing streams. On its fringes, where movement is slower, plants may gain a hold. Gorse and heather are common and even trees may grow. Out of the cover of this dense vegetation lizards and adders come to bask on hot rocks in the early summer sunshine. Reptiles are cold-blooded and need to warm themselves in this way before they can become fully active. Adders, or vipers (their other common name) are easily recognised by the dark zig-zag marking along the back but the overall colour of the animals is very variable. Dark, almost black specimens, with the zig-zag barely distinguishable, are quite common. Your chances of actually seeing these snakes, however, are small. Unless you

Valley of the Rocks, Lynton

Scree

56

Scree slope at Foreland Point

are quiet and stealthy an adder will detect the vibrations of your footsteps and will disappear into the undergrowth long before you are aware of its presence.

Adders are poisonous but their reputation is greatly exaggerated. Hardly more than a dozen people have died after being bitten by an adder in the past 70 years. Death is usually due to an allergic reaction to the venom, also a common reason for death in some cases after bee or wasp stings. The adder actually uses its poison as a very effective means of subduing active, fast-moving prey. It can stalk its prey and deliver the poisonous bite in a surprise attack and then track the dying animal at its leisure by following the scent-trail.

The rivers that flow to the sea through the spectacular scree-slope valleys are short but vigorous, tumbling swiftly over boulder-strewn beds. The Lyn valleys and Heddon Valley are, for the most part, clothed in woodlands of sessile oak, a tree that thrives on the thin, poor covering of soil. Rainfall on the high moors powers these rivers. Little more than 30 inches of rain a year falls at the coast but over 80 inches is usual on the high uplands in the heart of the moor. There is water enough at times to fuel devastating floods, capable of setting in motion gigantic boulders many tons in weight. In flood the Lyn rivers are an awesome sight; water roars and surges through the valleys and crashes over the many small falls. Yet when the water is low it gently

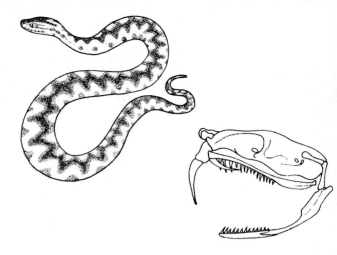

Adder's skull showing fang, replacement fang and hinged jaw. The poison is delivered down a tube in the fang. Worn fangs are quickly repl... and the jaw can be unhinged and opened very wide to enable the adder to sw... large preys

trickles and gurgles over its rocky bed giving no hint of its frightening potential.

To survive the swift currents and alternating episodes of torrent and calm, life in these rivers shelters beneath stones or seeks the relative safety of waters little affected by flood. Turn over any stone and there will be an explosion of frantic movement as creatures scuttle for safety. First out are the water

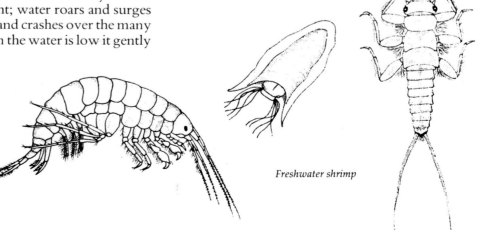

Freshwater shrimp

Watersmeet

shrimps, *Gammarus,* active and powerful swimmers that quickly find new places to hide. More wary of leaving the stone but running about trying to escape the light are the larvae of mayflies and stoneflies. Their streamlined, flattened body shape enables them to press close to the stone offering no projections which the current could pull at and so wash them away. Unable to escape are the larvae of black-flies and caddis flies, concealed in their protective cases which are cemented to the stone.

All these creatures fall prey to the dipper, a remarkable bird that walks or swims along the river bottom turning over pebbles in search of food. Under water the force of the current keeps the dipper submerged as it heads upstream against the current, shining silver from the air trapped around its body. Out of water it is a dumpy, blackish-brown bird with a conspicuous white bib. It crouches low and bobs constantly up and down on a rock or flies fast and low above the stream.

Fishes, too, take their toll of river life. Salmon and trout gulp down dislodged invertebrates and snatch mayfly larvae as they rise to the surface. Mayfly larvae feed on algae and can occur in huge numbers in fast-flowing streams. When the larvae are ready to moult into the winged adult form they divert respiratory air between the old and new cuticle until they rise, like corks, to the surface. Once on the surface it generally takes only a few seconds for the adult to burst free of its larval skin and take to the air, but this is when they are most vulnerable and when the big fish move in to snap them up. Those that escape, still an enormous number, will fly over the water in whirling mating swarms. These adults do not feed – they have no functioning mouth parts and have to live on the store of fat deposited when they were larvae. Their brief lives are devoted solely to reproduction.

Quieter reaches of water support the carnivorous larvae of damselflies. Two colourful species of damselfly, the banded demoiselle and the beautiful demoiselle, are common along the river at Heddon Valley. In summer the beautiful demoiselles flutter daintly over the water, the metallic blue wings of the male and iridescent green wings of the female sparkling like jewels. The male of the banded demoiselle has conspicuous purple-blue spots on each wing. During courtship the males perform aerial displays in small groups, flicking their spotted wings to attract a mate and to outshine their rivals. In the act of mating the damselfly male grasps the neck of the female with special claspers at the tip of his abdomen and the female curves up underneath him so that they form a circle. Banded demoiselle damselflies have the fascinating habit of crawling below water, the male still clasping the female, in order to lay their eggs. Demoiselles are territorial, dashing out from their waterside perches to chase off intruding males or to display to a passing female. They usually perch on the leaves of overhanging bushes or trees or the tall, leafy stems of streamside plants.

One of the plants to be found growing at the side of the stream is the tall, robust hemlock water dropwort, crowned with big, showy domes of white flowers. Each tiny flower in the flowerhead secretes copious quantities of nectar which is irresistible to insects. Large and small hoverflies, some shining copper or gold, others banded black and yellow in imitation of wasps, dart on and off the flowers, hovering momentarily before alighting. Flesh flies, dark and sombre, fly rapidly from flowerhead to flowerhead. The opportunities presented by so many insects crowding to this precious resource are not lost on predators. Hunting wasps swoop on unsuspecting flies, and crab spiders, camouflaged by their white colouring, lurk motionless among the flowers in wait for unwary prey. With legs outstretched, the spiders sit constantly alert, ready to deliver the single venomous bite that quickly subdues the struggles of their hapless victims. Even large insects can be easily overcome by these spiders: it is not unusual to find a butterfly or bee sitting on the flowers, quite dead but in perfect condition. The only sign of the spider's work will be two tiny puncture wounds in the head or thorax.

Where the river meets woodland, it is not uncommon for the crab spider's victim to be a silver washed fritillary butterfly. The silver washed fritillary is the largest and most handsome of our fritillaries. It has a wingspan of over 2½ inches and has a silvery sheen on the underside of its brown and black dappled wings, from which it derives its name. A woodland species, it is on the wing from July to September and can be seen in most Exmoor oak-woods, hawking up and down in rides and clearings. Like all fritillaries, it has a complicated life cycle. The female lays her eggs in crevices on the bark of oak trees. The caterpillars hatch out about two weeks later, eat their eggshells and promptly fall into an unbroken hibernation that lasts for up to eight months. Whey they awaken in the spring the caterpillars have to make the long journey down the tree trunk to the woodland floor where they search for the violets on which they feed.

In the same oak-woods may be found the purple hairstreak, a diminutive butterfly that tends to keep to the upper branches of oak trees and is, therefore, not often seen. It has a distinctive, fluttering flight but is never very active, coming down from the treetops only

Silver washed Fritillary
P. Wakely, Nature Conservancy Council

to feed from flowers in the woodland glades or to bask in patches of sunlight. It is a butterfly of ancient woodlands where there is little intensive management and where aged oaks are allowed to grow.

Most of the oak-woods on the steep, difficult slopes of the Exmoor coastal fringe favoured by the purple hairstreak have a continuous history dating back possibly 10,000 years. It was around this time that the first forests began to colonise the barren soil left by the retreating ice caps. Since then, despite exploitation by man, it is unlikely that these woods have ever been completely cleared or put under the plough. Until the coming of our age of metal and plastic, wood was a major commodity and a precious resource. Small parcels of woodland were cleared in rotation and it was only after twenty or thirty years of natural regeneration that a particular parcel was cleared again. But,

unlike today, clearance was not complete. Some trees, old and young, were always left standing to ensure a continuous and varied supply of timber. This method of management also ensured that an abundance of wildlife could survive because there was always another parcel of woodland nearby for species to move into. With their continuous history, ancient woodlands are extremely rich in wildlife. The woodlands of the Lyn valleys, Heddon Valley and possibly Woody Bay are all ancient and support a marvellous diversity of plant and animal life.

Several western or 'oceanic' plants grow in the Lyn valleys' woods. Irish spurge, common in Ireland and on the Atlantic coast of Europe, grows in Britain only here and around the Lizard peninsular in Cornwall; the pretty yellow-flowered Welsh poppy is abundant and grows as a true native in these woods. Other plants, such as wood stitchwort, primarily a northern species, are at the very southern limits of their range. There are also two extremely rare ferns growing on damp rocks shaded by the canopy of trees. The Tunbridge filmy fern and Wilson's filmy fern are tiny, paper-thin ferns that are easily mistaken for leafy mosses. Wilson's filmy fern is so rare that it is now given protection under the Wildlife and Countryside Act. Some trees, too, are unusual. Among the oak, ash and rowan can be found the whitebeam, a handsome small tree with large, toothed and densely white-felted leaves. Its clusters of white flowers in May are followed by dull orange berries in the autumn. There are many subspecies of whitebeam and one, frequent in the Lyn valleys, is special to Devon and known, appropriately, as the Devon whitebeam. The various subspecies are difficult to identify, even by the experts, and one large tree near the bridge at Watersmeet remains un-named to this day!

Whitebeam

The ancient woodlands of Exmoor are not without their birds to exploit the rich harvest of life. Parties of tits forage in the treetops for caterpillars and aphids, incessantly calling to each other in high-pitched twitters and nasal *'churrs'*. A short, piping *'chick'* gives away the presence of a nuthatch as it climbs the tree trunks in jerking hops, head first, upwards or downwards with equal facility. This attractive little bird with a slate-grey back and orange-brown belly has the habit of deliberately wedging nuts into crevices in bark and hammering them open with its powerful pointed bill. Scrubbier patches of woodland with a thick ground cover of bramble attract chiff-chaffs and willow warblers. Almost identical in appearance, these birds can only be distinguished reliably by their markedly different songs. The name of the chiff-chaff is derived from its repetitive two-note song. The willow warbler, in contrast, has a gentle song with a long, descending cadence that, perhaps more than any other bird song, epitomises the warmth and tranquillity of an English summer's day.

Sessile oak

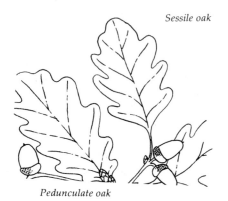

Pedunculate oak

Two strikingly handsome birds which also occur in the Exmoor woodlands are the pied flycatcher and the redstart. The pied flycatcher has only a tenuous hold in Exmoor's woods. It is very particular about its habitat and although it appears regularly on passage, if it is to breed it must be in an area with more than 40 inches of rainfall a year and often, though not always, it nests near water. The pied flycatcher is a very fickle bird, appearing in good numbers one year and not at all the next. Yet their very fickleness has made them highly prized 'specimens' and ornithologists have erected nest boxes in suitable woodlands to encourage them to nest. The black and white male is easily recognised as it flits from perch to perch catching insects in the air.

The redstart is a bird of open, sessile oak woodlands. Male redstarts need clear spaces beneath the trees to hawk for insects with their flycatcher-like flight. They also need a large 'showground' with good visibility to tempt their females with spectacular courtship flights. Both sexes have an unmistakable fiery rufous tail, and the male, with his dark grey back, black bib and deep orange belly is an extremely handsome creature. During courtship all this bright colouring is put to good effect when he dances before the female with a dazzling display of tail-fanning and wing-spreading.

As the small birds feed on the bounty of the woods, so the sparrowhawk wings its way in low, silent flight along the edges of the woodland, searching them out as his prey. The sparrowhawk is not a common bird in this part of Exmoor, but it is truly a woodland bird. It builds its nest high up in the branches of woodland trees and exhibits an astonishing agility in flight that enables it to twist and turn at great speed between the trees and bushes in pursuit of the birds on which it feeds.

In contrast, the buzzard, a more common raptor on Exmoor, uses the woods only for nesting and prefers to soar high above the moors and valleys, surveying the ground below for signs of carrion and prey. It also perches on fence posts and telegraph poles from where, with slow wingbeats, it launches on its low-level hunting flights. Because of this habit, the buzzard is one of the few birds of prey which will allow a close approach. A car is invaluable as the birds can often be seen on roadsides; provided you stay inside the car and don't venture too close, the buzzard will sit tight. While you admire his mottled brown plumage, his cruelly-curved beak and powerful yellow talons, he will study you with sharp eyes, ready to flap gently away at the slightest hint of danger.

The main prey of buzzards are rabbits. In the 1950s when the rabbit population was decimated by myxomatosis, buzzard numbers went into serious decline. Even now, when myxomatosis is no longer such a virulent disease, the buzzards' fortunes wax and wane in parallel with the scarcity or abundance of their rabbit prey. Despite the preference for rabbit, their diet is varied and they take small mammals, birds, insects, worms and carrion – for the most part sheep which have died on the moor. As a buzzard circles high in the sky it watches for signs of a carcase, with eyes eight times more acute than those of a human being.

What a view the high-flying buzzard must have as it wheels over the hills and valleys of Exmoor and traverses the great tracts of coastal heaths along the hog's-back cliffs. In early summer these heaths are ablaze with the purple blossom of bell heather and the yellow of western gorse. The coastal heaths stretch all the way from Combe Martin to the Foreland, unbroken except for an occasional parcel of

Bell heather

On warm summer days bumblebees search for nectar amongst the heath flowers and larks hang in the sky above, singing their endless song. Below, the sea is turquoise and sea birds wheel out from unseen ledges. For this glorious fringe of Exmoor harbours the only sea-bird colony of any size on the North Devon coast. Guillemots, razorbills, kittiwakes, fulmars and gulls all nest together on inaccessible cliffs near Woody Bay. It is impossible to see the colony from the cliffs and downright dangerous to try. Close views of the birds can best be had by taking the daily boat trip from Lynmouth during the early summer nesting season.

woodland. They are drier than the upland moors and the compact, dark-leaved bell heather replaces the tall-growing, robust common heather or ling. Within the influence of the sea there are patches of grass and bracken through which grow the tiny yellow flowers of tormentil, purple violets and scrambling clusters of small, white flowers of the heath bedstraw. It is quite possible that these grassy coastal heaths have never been wooded. If so, then like the ancient woodlands of the valleys, they have a continuous history that goes right back to the last Ice Age; they are probably among the very few remaining natural 'unimproved' grasslands in Britain.

Where the scree breaks through the cover of vegetation there is a profusion of sheep's sorrel with its small, arrow-shaped leaves and russet seed spikes. Sheep's sorrel and its larger relative, the common sorrel, are sometimes known as 'vinegar plants' because of the sharp, acid taste of their leaves. It is not an unpleasant taste, however, and the juice of the leaves has the peculiar property of causing a refreshing salivation. Farm hands used to chew the leaves to slake their thirst as they worked in hot, dusty fields during the summer.

Sheeps Sorrel   *P. Wakely, Nature Conservancy Council*

Sea birds favour this stretch of the coast simply because of an accident of geology. On most parts of the North Devon coast the rock strata are nearly vertical, or tend to angle forward and downward and easily break away from the cliff. Rockfalls are frequent and there are very few secure and stable rock ledges. Around Woody Bay, however, the layers of rock dip gently backwards and weather readily into a series of ledges, some broad, some narrow, but all relatively stable. These are ideal nesting sites for cliff birds.

Razorbills and guillemots lay their single egg each year directly on to the ledges, making no attempt to construct a nest. The razorbill prefers to lodge its egg in a crevice, where perhaps a little soil has collected, but the guillemot lays on the bare rock surface, relying on the shape of the egg to keep it in place on the ledge. The egg is markedly pear-shaped and this serves to roll it in a complete circle if it is ever dislodged, making it unlikely that the egg will be knocked accidentally off the nesting ledge.

Both the razorbill and guillemot are primarily fish eaters, though the razorbill has a more varied diet that includes molluscs and undersea worms. The birds fly out to sea on rapidly-beating, stubby wings which also propel them deep under water as they dive for prey. Both parents share the four weeks' incubation of the egg. After only a fortnight, even before they can fly properly, the young fledgelings are encouraged to jump off the ledges into the sea at high tide. They swim a mile or two off shore and one of the parents will continue to feed them until they are fully fledged.

Fulmars, which first arrived on the North Devon coast at Woody Bay in 1955, prefer ledges with some cover of vegetation. Kittiwakes, which began to breed here in 1970, construct a bracket nest composed of green algae and debris which is stuck to the rock face with excrement. On top of this messy foundation the birds make a final cup nest of mud and grass. New nests are built on top of old ones and in time the kittiwake sits on top of a 'skyscraper' of weed and dung! There are now almost 500 pairs of kittiwakes at Woody Bay and numbers are still increasing. Kittiwakes are beautiful gulls, superficially similar to the other common species but they have black legs and a yellow bill with a vivid orange gape. They are also more oceanic than the other gulls, spending long periods at sea outside the breeding season. They feed from the surface or by plunging into the water, catching small fish and floating animal plankton as well as hawking for insects while on the wing.

Tiger beetle.
A ferocious bright-green predatory beetle common on Exmoor.
Long-legged and fast-running, has a buzzing flight

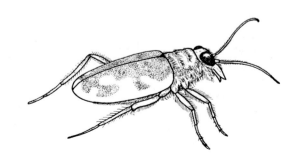

BADGER BOOKS

The Heritage series looks at Devon as it is today and as it once was. The books attempt to preserve memories of bygone eras and also to record our County's history, both ancient and modern.

All the Heritage books are profusely illustrated with both new and many charming old photographs and prints, plus maps of the areas covered.

"Wildlife – Mammals" by Trevor Beer £1.95

A clear, concise description accompanied by the author's illustrations of the principal mammals to be found in the Devon Countryside, from Red Deer to Pygmy Shrews.

"The Cruel Coast of North Devon" by Michael Nix £1.95

Not merely a catalogue of shipwrecks, Michael Nix describes the agony of disaster and the efforts made to avert it from early lighthouses and lifesaving equipment down to the present day, ending with the wreck *Johanna* off Hartland point.

"Back Along the Lines – North Devon's Railways" by Victor Thompson £1.95

Not written for railways enthusiasts alone, but a charmingly worded reconstruction of the history of the branch lines that did so much to improve communications throughout North Devon. Sadly, all save the line to Exeter have disappeared but fond memories linger on.

"Villages of North Devon" £1.95
"Market Towns of North Devon" by Rosemary Anne Lauder £1.95

Of interest to visitor and local inhabitant alike, the author has travelled throughout North Devon and describes in "Villages" those with something to offer in the way of history, or picturesque appearance, or true Devonian character. In "Market Towns" Barnstaple, Bideford, Hatherleigh, Holsworthy, Okehampton and Torrington are in turn studied with a history and a modern profile of each town.

"Lundy – Puffin Island" by Rosemary Anne Lauder

A discovery of Devon's mystical island, loved by all who know it, yet relatively unknown to many Devonians.

"Along the Shore" by Mike Towns

An exploration of North Devon's beautiful yet rugged coastline, its formation and its wildlife.

"A Herbal Folklore" by Anne-Marie Lafont

Fascinating remedies and old recipes from country kitchens in the days when the plants of hedgerow and garden were put to many and varied uses.

Also available:

"Vanished Houses of North Devon" by Rosemary Anne Lauder £1.95

The story of six former mansions – Stevenstone, Eggesford, Dunsland, Annery, Yeo Vale and Winscott – now gone for ever.

"Tarka Country" by Trevor Beer £1.95

Follows the story of Henry Williamson's famous otter "Tarka and his joyful water-life and death in the Country of the Two Rivers."

"Anthology for North Devon" £1.95

A compilation of old and new – poetry, prose and photographs including the Devonshire dialect.